HERE'S WHAT PEOPLE ARE SAYING ABOUT *AND: THE RESTORATIVE POWER OF LOVE IN AN EITHER/OR WORLD* AND FELICIA MURRELL...

My dear friend and exemplar asks, "Who are you in the eyes of Love?" Through memories made vivid and her poetic treasury, Felicia Murrell gently guides me (yet again) back into Love's embrace. There, in the "both/and" of my own real life—wounds and wonders, beauty and affliction—I remember again, I am beloved. I often forget. But Felicia's kind voice represents, for me, what a healed conscience can become in full bloom. I will wear this book out.

—*Bradley Jersak*
Principal, St. Stephen's University
Author, *Out of the Embers*

Felicia Murrell understands *and*. In her heartfelt, poetic narrative, *And: The Restorative Power of Love in an Either/Or World*, she takes you deep into the heart of a Love that insists that we are not either/or but both/and, exposing the "isms" that seek to divide us. She demonstrates that in the midst of the messiness of life, Love calls to us to love.

—*Fr. Richard Rohr, OFM*
Author, *The Divine Dance* and *The Universal Christ*

In *AND: The Restorative Power of Love in an Either/Or World*, Felicia Murrell gives us a gift of love we are meant to experience. If taken slowly, thoughtfully, bravely, this book will heal us, individually and together. Weaving together poetry and prose, Felicia shares vulnerably, guiding us from her own story to encourage, challenge, confront, and call us to love. This beautiful, healing book takes us on an embodied journey, inviting us to fully inhabit our humanity, to defy our divides, to live as one.

—*Susan Carson*
Podcaster, speaker, and author
Rooted (IN): Thriving in Connection with God, Yourself, and Others

In this well-written meditation on love, Felicia Murrell offers us a resting place, a wake-up call, a soul-quickening. This book is luminous and wise.

—*Mirabai Starr*
Teacher; author, *Wild Mercy*

With the brilliance of a writer/poet, the kind ferocity of a lamb/lion, and a flaming sword that cuts both ways, Felicia Murrell has gifted us this treasure of authenticity and wisdom. If you have no intention of being confronted, challenged, and changed, I would avoid this book.

—*Paul Young*
Author, *The Shack* and *Eve*

Felicia Murrell has created a stunning work of contemplative jazz, reflections that invite us into the fullness of our shared humanity through an embodied contemplation, willingness to unknow, and the courage to let love lead us into a larger imagination. *And: The Restorative Power of Love in an Either/Or World* is a kaleidoscope of hope in a world that often feels torn by the controlling certitudes and safe binaries we cling to. This is a book you will want to savor slowly and digest over a lifetime.

—*Brie Stoner*
Musician, author, and artist

In her beautiful new book, *And: The Restorative Power of Love in an Either/Or World*, Felicia Murrell does not just offer you well-chosen and beautifully arranged words: she offers you her soul, and it is a wise soul, a deep soul, a creative and generous soul. In lucid prose, accessible poetry, and prayers that welcome you whatever your creed, she is like a pathfinder who has explored the world and returned to show us a way to what matters most. This book is a rare gift, best if read slowly and savored like fresh home-baked bread and a rich, balanced wine.

—*Brian D. McLaren*
Author, *Faith After Doubt*

AND: THE RESTORATIVE POWER OF LOVE

IN AN EITHER/OR WORLD

FELICIA MURRELL

WHITAKER HOUSE

AND
The Restorative Power of Love in an Either/Or World

feliciamurrell@gmail.com

ISBN: 979-8-88769-140-4
eBook ISBN: 979-8-88769-141-1
Printed in the United States of America
© 2024 by Felicia Murrell

Illustrations by Jonathon Stalls of intrinsicpaths.com.

Whitaker House
1030 Hunt Valley Circle
New Kensington, PA 15068
www.whitakerhouse.com

LC record available at https://lccn.loc.gov/2023040790
LC ebook record available at https://lccn.loc.gov/2023040791

1 2 3 4 5 6 7 8 9 10 11 W 32 31 30 29 28 27 26 25 24

A heart in communion with Love is a heart that is free.

This is for all the free ones and the ones on their journey.
May all be free.

CONTENTS

The author's heart is to tell her real, raw story. Thus, this book includes minimal explicit language and is not intended for all audiences.

INTRODUCTION

This is not material to speed-read through. Certainly, you could read it all in one sitting, but it's probably best when digested in chunks. Read a piece, and let it marinate. Perhaps grab your journal, write what comes to mind, or sit with Love inside the words and what stirs from them. Then take a walk. Come back to the words and read some more. I want this offering to be something for you to really take in and sit with. If these words and this book can, in any way, be bread and wine, then take and eat. This is my body, given for you.

—Felicia Murrell

FOREWORD

Reading Fe's words, I am challenged and alive. It's as if I have curled up on her couch. I'm chatting with her, talking about all the things, hearing her takes.

If listening is an entryway into love, then this book is an offer to listen. There is such vulnerability to Fe's words.

Fe offers us an invitation, an opportunity to feel and experience life through her words. Not all are in a place to hear and receive, but there is a body of people out there who are in such a place—those on the edges of leaving the institutional church; or those who have left but are still holding on to ideals; those who are just waking up, still wiping the crust from their eyes as they slowly open. This book is for them.

For those who are already wondering, for those who crave guidance and an offer into thinking more deeply, this book is a guide, a place to ponder, to sit with things, to aid in discovery. There are no lanes declared here, just thoughts, suggestions, and experiences that make us wonder. For those who don't have space or places to ask, talk, and verbally process, this is a much-needed book. This book allows a journey with doubt but does not make it the destination.

The basis of this book is love. It's who Fe is, the life she has lived, what she has made of it, and who she has become in it. Fe is a gift.

Not everybody has a way with words or putting thoughts and ideas out there that feed souls. Fe does. It's the nature of who she is. It's how she nurtures herself and those around her. If I didn't have Fe in my life, I would want the chance to read her on the page. Fe braves the roller coaster of writing, holding ground when emotions come. And now, through the pages of this book, we all have the chance to give the gift of her to others. What a beautiful opportunity to share in Fe's journey.

If I had a friend who was on a journey of waking up, of seeing things in a different light, of embracing the more, I would hand them a copy of this book and say, "Here is the gift of a conversation you might not have a safe place to have, a chance to answer some questions that cause you to ask more questions. Here is the gift of someone's experience with Love. May it transform you as it transformed her."

—*Katie Christian*
Friend and blogger at Our Highway Five

PREFACE

None of the things I do is a calling for me. If it all fell away tomorrow, it wouldn't upend my world.

The significance of my existence is not attached to any lofty purpose or high calling.

I exist to exist. I exist to love. I exist to receive Love as a continuous experience in my heart, to live in it and give it away to others.

I am bound in life to the sacredness of creation. I am attached to the idea that people, created in the image of Love, are born to live free, to live loved, and to be love.

However I can order my day to participate with Love in ushering in that freedom, for myself and for others, that is the Way of Love for me.

What is mine to do? To *live and move and have my being* as I consciously participate in the flow of Love.

People spend their lives chasing and pursuing the thing that completes them or makes them happy.

Pause. Listen to your heart.

Who are you before the world of ambition tried to define you for you? Who are you in the eyes of Love?

Apart from someone else or something else shaping the framework of your existence, who are you? Without the apostrophe of someone else's role and function, who are you? Why do you exist?

When I surrendered my ambitions, my vain imaginations of conjured realities and expectations of the shape and form in which my dreams were supposed to manifest themselves, it freed the Beloved from my demand that the Holy Three perform in a certain way to meet my expectations.

Now, I'm learning to live in contentment, drawing significance and value from simply living loved. And leaning my head upon the Beloved's breast, my heart is stirred. "Dearest Beloved, what would you have a little girl from C-town say to a nation that you so dearly love?"

May the eyes and ears of our hearts hear nothing but the tender whispers of Divine Love.

GATEWAY TO KNOWING:

I never questioned the world in which I grew up. I followed the rhythms set for me by those around me, understanding the world and how to situate myself in it through the lenses and lives of those in authority over me. I learned to orient myself to their whims and flights of fancy. I learned when it was necessary to shrink myself, to make myself disappear.

In the small rural North Carolina town of my youth, Blacks lived on one side of the tracks and whites on the other. The grocery stores, diners, convenience store, post office, schools, and gas stations were across the tracks, on the white side of town. On our side of the tracks, only a small store my great-uncle owned, the candy lady's home, and three predominantly Black churches were easily accessible to us. Even in the late seventies and on into the early eighties, we stepped off the sidewalk when white people walked past, turning our gaze downward or to the side, never making direct eye contact. We paused our movement to let them enter establishments first, and on the rare occasion that we got to eat at Jones's (the local café), we called in our food order and then crossed the railroad tracks to the café's back door, where we gave our money to the one Black worker and retrieved our greasy hamburgers and hot dogs in a small paper sack. Nothing about this life seemed abnormal. This was our story.

As a child, I existed in a world of play, family, and church—and then I went to school, where I interacted with white people for the first time. And with play being such an integral part of the world in which I grew up, it never dawned on me that asking my white classmates, "Can I come over to your house to play?" was taboo.

I was five. What did I know about situational ethics and contextual relationships?

More than four decades have passed since I posed that question, but I'll never forget the replies of those twin sisters in my kindergarten class. One shook her head and said, "You're our secret. We can't play with you when we're not at school." "Why?" I asked in five-year-old naïveté. The other sister answered, "'Cause you're a nigger. My grandma don't want us playing with niggers."

I shrugged off their comments, and we continued our play as if nothing cruel had transpired, yet indelible ink wrote across the pages of my heart in crisp kindergarten crayon scribble: *There is something bad about me.* I was special enough to play with at school but not good enough to be invited into their home. That day, the measuring stick known as comparison, etched with varying degrees of insignificance and unworthiness, formed in the recesses of my soul. And long into adulthood, I would constantly be measuring myself by how well I adapted and fit into whiteness.

By the time that happened at school, I had more questions burrowing into my little five-year-old brain than I knew what to do with. Why did people stop talking and stare at us with mean glares if we went through the front door at Jones's? Why did we have to go to the back door? Why did they only have one Black person working across town? Why was the dance studio in our town only for white girls? Why did we tame our joy and become quiet in the presence of white people? Why wouldn't the twins' grandmother let me play at their house? And why did that n-word feel bad? Why? Why? Why?

There were so many things that didn't make sense, but the tracks stilled my questions. Years later, Dr. Barbara Holmes would help me understand that the framework for my story has always been a Blackness shaped in response to whiteness, particularly as one raised in the rural South, where our story was formed on lynching trees that bore strange fruit: heightened awareness, cautious docility, and silence.

No one talked about race. No one expressed discontent or named things aloud. No one mentioned the way things were. We didn't buck the system. We kept our heads down and did what we were supposed to do. Success and advancement were others' stories, for people across town on the other side of the tracks. We were to stay in our place and follow the natural order of things, which I did until I no longer could.

Like matryoshka dolls nesting within one another, my story as a small child was a fragmented, compartmentalized part of a larger narrative. In the shadow of dominant voices, my story felt less essential, even unnecessary. Without a clear understanding of the whole, my story was incomplete. But my story was all I knew until I was exposed to other stories.

My grandmother left the Deep South before I was born, migrating north to Washington, DC. There, she and my grandfather carved out a life of joy amid toil. And, in the summer, my brother and I were fortunate enough to ride the Greyhound bus, carrying foil-wrapped ham sandwiches and cold fried chicken, to join them. Our grandmother was intentional about exposure. She structured our summers with visits to the zoo, museums, the Mint, and the Capitol; swimming; and fountain wading at Union Station. She introduced us to the performing arts. Without us ever boarding a plane, my grandmother made sure we knew the world was bigger than Clayton, North Carolina. There were other stories, and while these outings merely served as introductions, she helped us see the possibility of these stories being available to us as well. My grandmother's intentionality gifted me with points of connection to a larger story beyond my narrow worldview.

When we remain stuck in the loop of our story without consideration of other stories, particularly when *our* is framed in (or lived in response to) a Eurocentric, patriarchal, dominant paradigm as the standard of measurement for all other stories, we are left with an incomplete model.

Exposure to other stories is an invitation, a gateway to knowing. But it's merely that—an opportunity to know. A welcoming and acceptance of diversity may create familiarity, but it's not the same as knowing. Deep, intimate knowing empowers agency, offers reciprocity, and, through mutuality, affords us the opportunity to be the custodians of our own story without being othered as an aside or a concession to dissent.

From kindergarten through university, I played, studied, and participated in groups and teams alongside white people, but there was no interest in knowing. I've worked with white people in the workplace, and I have gone to church with white people for most of my adult life. Some would even say we were friends, but there has been no interest in knowing. We've mingled contextually, but not with the kind of knowing that re-members, re-joins, re-collects. Any story without deep, intimate knowing leaves the parties untouched.

Cynthia Bourgeault writes, "The energetic bandwidth in which the heart works is intimacy, the capacity to perceive things from the inside by coming into sympathetic resonance with them...The heart takes its bearings directly from the whole."[1]

Intimacy—into me you see.

Empathy is imagined embodiment, placing myself into the story of another and gazing through their eyes: seeing their lived experience; thinking for perhaps the first time how that person would feel encountering certain things—certain policies, language, or interactions; receiving their pain, but not

---

1. Cynthia Bourgeault, *The Heart of Centering Prayer: Nondual Christianity in Theory and Practice* (Boulder, CO: Shambhala, 2016), 120.

through a myopic imagining that one might have apart from this deep intimacy.

Empathy transcends the imagining of a life we never have to personally live, making the kindred connection that allows our hearts to break open to the painful, fearful, or even joyous experiences of another in such a deep way that we can never again unknow what we've come to know. Empathy fosters deep knowing.

And there, in the clear-eyed seeing of who we are to one another— interconnected, where nothing lives separate and distinct from the other, where there is uniqueness of person-hood and space for the ways in which we vary and are different from one another—is the invitation into the possibility of the moment.

Intimate, empathetic knowing allows for *sympathetic resonance*, a melding of hearts forged in the weaving of stories and lives together until there is only the story, which is the restoration of all things as all embrace divine unity in the encounter of Love.

Love is infinite, and in the bounty of Love, we are held, and we are known.

Within the frame of both/and, our story and other stories weave together in the native language of *be*-ing, which is oneness. This is not a oneness that spiritually bypasses the beauty of particularity, but one that harmoniously holds the complexity of all things in their distinct and unique speci-ficity. It doesn't require people to become *pure, white light* or a blob of detached personhood to reach the highest level of homeostasis or enlightenment. Instead, it honors the color-ful spectrum of humanity without trying to erase or deny its biodiversity. Oneness undergirds distinction, diversity, and multiplicity. In this unity that celebrates all difference, we can each live into our full humanity, embracing our truest, most authentic selves, *and* give ourselves to the well-being of others in perichoretic mutuality without fear of absorption or domination.

The image of Russian nesting dolls, all carved from the same wood, shaped the same, and painted the same, feels fitting when thinking of where we are in the world today. Fear rises as some rush to erase or reimagine history. It's a world where calls for peace and unity feel weaponized. Colorblindness replaces clear-eyed seeing, lost amid our need for ease, for sameness. Pressure mounts to decry the harmonious voices, exclaiming in concert for a chord of sameness. Same feels safe. Same feels comfortable. It requires no effort and little thought. Same can be achieved on autopilot. The appeal of sameness is that it doesn't require us to be present or aware in the way that is required when wading through the messy complexity of being human and being in relationship with other messy, complex humans.

Could this be why we need to produce maps to explain the mysteries of our complexity as humans? We erect pillars of certainty—tidy, neat guideposts that reduce our vibrant existence into small, static pictures. Maps are fixed and finite; once we've memorized our mapped route, we often navigate unconsciously—until change, like a global pandemic, creates unfamiliar detours.

What if the Universe is not asking for yet another map to attempt to make sense of the world as we know it? What if the tension is an invitation to let go and allow mystery without attempting to quantify or explain it? What if we surrendered to change, to this invitation into a new story, one not dominated by Eurocentric patriarchal rationalization? Like a singular wave rising up and out of a larger body of water, my story blends into our collective story, yielding to the change of our energetic makeup. "By being receptive to the things that we don't understand," writes Dr. Barbara

Holmes in *Crisis Contemplation: Healing the Global Village,*
"we fling open the center of our being to the mysteries of the
Divine."[2]

All that you touch

You Change.

All that you Change

Changes you.

The only lasting truth

Is Change.

God Is Change.[3]

How do we honor our uniqueness while destroying vary-
ing degrees of separation? How do we move toward each
other in love, the truth of our authentic power? Perhaps, we
welcome change instead of resisting it. To expand my worl-
dview beyond the paradigm of Southern, Christian, rural
or working poor to a larger cosmic frame that is inclusive,
universal, affirming, and accepting, I needed to see the parts
and the whole in all their majestic splendor and their messy
complexity.

Transcendence is not a denial or detachment from my
story or our story. It is an arduous commitment to truth-tell-
ing; to fully seeing; to empathetic listening that requires the
work of living and *be*-ing in the world; of deep, intimate
knowing; of moving beyond our theories and maps into
relationship building. This is not a quick work, nor is it an
easy work. The work is rife with tension and discomfort and
necessitates patience, time, humility, and kindness.

---

2. Barbara Holmes, *Crisis Contemplation: Healing the Wounded Village*
(Albuquerque, NM: CAC Publishing, 2021), 134.
3. Octavia E. Butler, *Parable of the Sower* (New York: Open Road Integrated
Media, 2012), chapter 1.

Perhaps Love is inviting us to embrace fluidity, to ebb and flow, to move with the current, to shapeshift in ways that are no longer disjointed, fragmented, or separated into neat, tidy categories. Bodies of water are always changing. Unimpeded, ocean water spills into gulfs. Gulfs spill into rivers. Rivers spill into lakes. Lakes spill into tributaries. All are commingling as one, interdependent, interconnected, yet distinct in their purpose—just as our stories are commingled, interconnected, interdependent, spilling over and into one another, back and forth in unity.

Much time has passed since George Floyd was murdered, since books by Black people rocketed to the top of the *New York Times* best-seller list, since corporations made anti-racist statements declaring *Black Lives Matter*, and people turned their social media profiles black in solidarity with the suffering.

What has changed? In you, in me, in the world...what has changed?

Did we rush too quickly to fix, to absolve ourselves of discomfort, to avoid the pain caused by a long history of messes made, realities ignored? Did we learn how to be sad together, to grieve with, or just be—to allow the weight of the moment to be its own master class—or have we rushed in, brandishing our savior capes, to plant a chair over the poop so our houses have an appearance of ordered cleanliness regardless of the smell?

I am a product of the South. I have stood in fields where my enslaved ancestors fled through trees while being chased by dogs and men with guns. I've stood in fields where war was fought, where decisions were made as to whether a being was a person or property. I've stood in blood-stained fields as a living, breathing witness to right appearance and right belief as ideals that are more important than the right of people to freely exist in their own skin.

I've known of bankers, judges, teachers, preachers—people who serve and smile by day, who gather around burning crosses in hooded white robes at night, and sometimes by day, with their wives and children. Picnics in hand, they take pictures by charred bodies swinging from trees, smug in the rightness of it all.

The right to pursue. The right to chase. The right to end a life for any reason they deemed appropriate. A rightness that sadly still hums through many police forces in the United States today.

As a child of the South, I lived in the fear that reverberated from my family's muscle memory, a fear that ordered my coming and going, my way to be in the world, demanding that I be small, invisible, that I shrink myself to the tiniest possible existence so I wouldn't be next: The next one to die. The next one to be raped or maimed.

Even when the white hooded robe made its way to the back of people's closets and lynching and cross burning were no longer a thing, in the South, we knew there were still ways to be lynched, still ways to be railroaded, still police willing to carry out long-held beliefs.

What is a reckoning without truth-telling, without acknowledging what has shaped us? Have we really slowed down enough to hear in the time that has passed since George Floyd was murdered? In that span of days, have we made space for people to vent and unburden their insides without crowding out discomfort—theirs and ours?

Pus draining from old wounds is a necessary thing to stave off infection. But not everyone can tolerate open sores.

Phobias and -isms have no place in the labor of Love. Therefore, it's imperative to know who the healers are. Who are those unfazed by gore that know how to love with strong stomachs?

Who has learned to handle the gruesome, to sit in the discomfort of their own pain, to allow space for others to live in theirs?

These touches of love that bind us to one another, this turning toward one another—this is the Way of Love. This is our way forward to the restoration and renewal of all things.

We think we have many problems, but we really have only one: a lack of love.

The thing is,

we've got to feel the pain to heal it and then

we've got to heal.

Pain demands we pick a side,

but we don't have to.

We can choose to side with love

and love sees fully.

Love is inclusive of both the victim and the perpetrator.

In our black and white,

right or wrong,

polarized society,

we demand allegiances

and then we castigate or accept others

based on their loyalty to their ideals

instead of loving them

for their humanity.

We all have the potential within us

to do depraved things

(*"Wretched man that I am"*[4])

It doesn't mean our depraved actions define us.

---

4. Romans 7:24.

It means we need Love to deliver us from evil,

and sometimes that evil lurks within.

When Love transforms our heart,

our actions align with the truth of our being

and we remember that which we already are:

the very good of God's creation,

created in the image

and likeness of Love.

"CHRIST BEFORE COLOR..."

I guess that's what the Ku Klux Klan thought too. And now that we've addressed this low-level attempt at spiritual bypassing, I'm pounding my palm against the wall with the duality. We gon' literally die on the poles of extreme opposites.

It's both/and.

BOTH. AND.

Racism IS most definitely systemic.

AND the fear, insecurities, and incorrect interpretation of "subdue the earth,"[5] which has led to a patriarchal obsession with dominance (of people, places, creation, and things), is very much a heart issue that has to be transformed through an experiential knowledge of Love.

---

5. See Genesis 1:28.

Dualism does not resolve tension; it only furthers our divide.

Yes, the laws can be changed. But who will change them if not people whose hearts are transformed? Who will abide by those changed laws if not people whose hearts and goodwill are motivated by Love?

We need both. Don't settle for either/or.

Educate. Legislate. And trust Spirit for the part we as a society can't do, which is heart transformation.

Am I more aware of the oppressed and the marginalized than I was six months ago?

Am I more loving than I was six months ago? Am I more forgiving than I was six months ago?

If hell is a state of mind created by the illusion of Love's absence, then heaven is the peaceful contentment of living, moving, and having my being in Love.

How does participating with Love aid in alleviating fear—society's and my own?

No one wants to be deemed a racist. But saying you're not a racist isn't enough.

We all need to unlearn learned myths—half-truths and falsities that have been perpetuated to create power, class, and privilege, to justify domination and create structures tailored to the advancement of some above others.

When we've acknowledged our privilege (which we all have, in one way or another), how do we move beyond racial superiority and integrate our holistic values in a way that doesn't advocate segregation or assimilation?

Cis white conservative patriarchy is not the only mirror for Divine Love.

I know we've all been colonized to believe assimilation is the only way to God. But who are we to say someone does not bear the Image because it's not our idea of the Image?

Tactics of shame create alliances with evil that keep us separated, hiding from ourselves and others instead of speaking to the good of our connection and interdependence.

Free people to be who they feel called to be. No one has the right to police the personhood of another.

A REFLECTION AS I SIT IN PRIVILEGE AWAY FROM TRAVESTY AND DESPAIR

I think the broad sweeping generalizations on both sides are killing us all.

And the evil one stands on the sidelines, laughing, feeling victorious because he has orchestrated hate, discord, division, fear, and tension among members of the human race, using pain, fear, and blame to target and destroy the beloved community.

But instead of recognizing the real enemy, we keep fighting ourselves.

As a race of people, we've made "winning" about dominating and control instead of living peaceably among all in submission and deference to one another.

Our suspicions and lack of trust beckon us to create hierarchies that control, maim, and keep people in their place.

We emasculate people we deem are a threat to our power, using dominance to force compliance.

As a society, we've made life about being right instead of being loved.

Grief shrivels the heart, closing it like a tightly budded rose. And as with a rose, there's always the risk of getting pricked. But somewhere inside of grief, I discovered a choice. I could continue to resist, or I could allow Love to break open my tightly budded heart despite the risk.

Untended grief can turn sharp and painful, erupting unbidden—by any means necessary—to pierce the conscience and burst the bubble of deception that shrouds those who refuse to allow grief its say. When no place is allowed for grief, there is no comfort, only pain, void, and loss.

Grief will have a voice, whether in a healthy manner, such as lament, or in the war cry of, *"Vengeance is mine; I will repay."*⁶ While every destructive expression of anger comes with an invitation from the Divine to experience love in that area, the present kumbaya illusion of peace, peace (calls for unity), and "all is well" is unsustainable.

As a woman clothed in Black skin facing all kinds of prejudices and hostilities, I could tell you story after story after story upon which we could sit and grieve. My lived reality is one that does not allow me to be passive or in denial. So, I live in a liminal space, betwixt and between, at a threshold of something imaginable but not yet. I live deeply connected to Love and my union with all creation, still profoundly moved by the crimes against humanity and my body identification. And while I mourn and am deeply grieved when someone chooses violence, exclusion, apathy, or hate as their expression of fear and doubt, my own journey with Love allows me to be patient enough to believe that Lovingkindness will one day reach every stony heart.

---

6. Romans 12:19 (KJV); see also Deuteronomy 32:35.

What I realize is that if I never grieve the injustices against my personhood, I will rob my soul of the necessary path it needs to experience transformational alchemy. And I'll never be able to integrate what my heart knows to be true: "Liberation is the opportunity for every human, no matter their body, to have unobstructed access to their highest self, for every human to live in radical self-love."[7]

Before liberation, we grieve. We acknowledge. We tell the truth. Passivity and denial won't work here. We have to honor the pain. We cannot rationalize it away, teach it away, philosophize it away, or religion it away. We have to turn and stare the hairy monster in the face. "Oh, hey. I see your jagged edges, like glass, that cut deep. I see the ways in which I have embodied violence against myself and others." I was them. I am them.

There is freedom in accepting all of me—every mistake I've made, every willful participation with domination, power, and violence—not as an excuse for my jagged edges, but as an invitation to return to myself, to offer an apology, to make amends, and to own the places where I've caused harm or been harsh. This is the freedom I've found in grief's discomfort: to stare the naked truth in the face; to see it, hear it, and embrace it without collapsing into the ground under the weight of my ugly parts.

This is the beauty of the rose's fragrance as it unfurls.

People are like glorious works of stained glass, a mix of vibrant colors and mosaic complexities.

I can't help but wonder how many times the glassmakers cut themselves before they learned to handle the cut pieces with delicacy. Learning how to handle grief delicately takes that same kind of patience.

---

7. Sonya Renee Taylor, *The Body Is Not an Apology* (Oakland, CA: Berrett-Koehler, 2021), 135.

*"Honor **all** people, love the family of believers, fear God, honor the king."*[8]

The issue of the sanctity of life goes beyond who is right and who is wrong. It goes beyond who provoked an argument, who started it, or who deserves what. The issue of life is one of honor, one of value, one of significance.

My gut feels the pain, anguish, anger, and inner turmoil of my people. I imagine that Martin Luther King Jr. was also a feeler. I find myself aspiring to his view and belief that darkness cannot drive out darkness. Only light can do that. And hate cannot drive out hate. Only love can do that.[9]

A dichotomy exists in a world that continues to have such a low view of humanity. My heart breaks at that. I want to look my sons in the face—no, I NEED to look my sons in the face and tell them to embrace forgiveness and, most of all, put on love.

But I cannot. I need them to first feel their grief, to rage, to feel the width and depth and charge of their anger, to locate the feeling of despair in their body.

I will not participate in quenching emotions of negation because purity culture has socialized us to rush to unity at the cost of myself

---

8. First Peter 2:17 (NET).
9. Martin Luther King Jr., *Where Do We Go from Here: Chaos or Community?* (Boston, MA: Beacon, 1968), 65.

and embrace shallow forgiveness that does not lead to heart change.
I will not.

We must wait, like midwives.

We must sit, like death doulas.

We must allow the energies to have their say.

We must.

And then, after lament, we move to alignment.

My child

my child

how I weep for thee.

Seven shots in the back.

Eight minutes and forty-six seconds on the neck.

I once pulled you from my breast,

sated and milk drunk,

you lolled against my skin,

my nipple elongated from suction,

your mouth dewy from sustenance.

The quiet of the moment, a holy hush

sacred as our hearts beating as one.

I wonder when they killed you

if you felt my love.

Did it ebb into you as life eked out of you?

Blood seeping from your wounds as easily as the milk that flowed
from my breast when you were small.

My child

my child

how I weep for thee:

your personhood,

your safety,

your humanity.

It took a village to raise you,

a tribe to feed you.

Nurtured on momma nems,

held by the strength of curved backs and cramped hands,

did you know in that moment that you weren't alone?

Could you feel the strength of love?

Could you see your ancestors as you joined the martyrs killed by
hate?

Were the other victims of brutality welcoming you at the gate?

Trayvon, Freddie, Philando, Tamir, Sandra, Breonna, Ahmaud,
Rayshard—

Who among them stood sentry at the portal?

Who saw the glint in your eyes,

the gleam in your smile?

Who noticed your easy gait,

marveled at your innocence and wondered how in the hell it
could ever be misconstrued as a threat?

My child

my child

how I weep for thee.

I beat my breasts that you once suckled,

now empty

dried up

tired, forlorn.

There are no words for this injustice:

I hunted like animals

Killed in the streets.

My child

my child

how I weep for thee.

May the earth speak your truth.

May the rain cry your tears.

May the birds hum your life's song.

And may we one day dance when the killing stops.

But until then

...arrest the cops.

Empty wombs,

filled tombs,

and still no one offers answers for this injustice.

My child
my child
how I weep for thee.

You tell me you're pro-life,
but you're also pro-death penalty:
people getting "what they deserved."

In your archaic language,
they
reap what they sow.

Now tell me:
Where is the grace in that?
Where is the God who pays the laborer of the last hour
the same as the laborer of the first?

Where is the Love that gives rise to
One plants
Another waters
Another harvests

But God gives the increase?

Where is the mercy,
the *chesed*,
the lovingkindness?

Where in the face of sanctioned murder
is "Father, forgive me,
I might have this wrong"?

Humility drowned out by power,
swept under by bravado and righteousness,
lost in translation on the tongues of saviors—
who know nothing of saving—
caught up in domination's energy,
perpetuating wars and mass genocides
to satiate the call to conquer
Will that call ever be silenced?
When it does quiet,
what will we hear in the space between?

The heartbeat of mercy:
Father, forgive them.
For they know not what they do
… … …or maybe they do.

Red tape on our mouths to save the babies

Laugh lines, firm brows

A nod of the head,

overseeing the execution of prisoners on death row

So high and mighty,

we determine who deserves an opportunity to live and who doesn't.

In the words of our own King:

Woe to you, teachers of the law and Pharisees, you hypocrites! You shut the door of the kingdom of heaven in people's faces… You travel over land and sea to win a single convert, and when you have succeeded, you make them twice as much a child of hell as you are. Woe to you, blind guides!…You blind fools!…You blind guides! You strain out a gnat but swallow a camel. Woe to you, teachers of the law and Pharisees, you hypocrites! You clean the outside of the cup and dish, but inside they are full of greed and self-indulgence. Blind Pharisee! First clean the inside of the cup and dish, and then the outside also will be clean. Woe to you, teachers of the law and Pharisees, you hypocrites! You are like whitewashed tombs, which look beautiful on the outside but on the inside are full of the bones of the dead and everything unclean. In the same way, on the outside you appear to people as righteous but on the inside you are full of hypocrisy and wicked-ness. (Matthew 23:13–28 NIV)

May the scales fall from our eyes and our hearts be enlarged with compassion.

May *the other* become *us* and may our scarcity mindset and fear of loss of power give way to generosity and equality.

Yes, let's help other countries. There's more than enough.

Yes, let's champion the unborn *and* the incarcerated on death row. There's more than enough for both.

Let's stop talking from our heads while sitting on our watoosies.

Let's stop swinging from the poles, lost in the tension of opposites, and find balance in humility, understanding, and listening.

Even when we're uncomfortable with someone else's lifestyle, can we choose quiet over condemnation?

Take a day and experience the injustice of the oppressed.

Ivory-castle ideas that haven't been forged in the fire will break under pressure of sustained heat.

Justice is love, lived in our actions and acknowledgment of humanity, no matter how alike or different that human is.

Justice is right alignment. Every person on the planet has the right to exist in their own skin and to walk out their journey with the Divine in their own way without my policing their path based on my agreement with their decisions or my own personal beliefs.

How uncomfortable do my ideas make you?

Can you challenge the worldview of your own, "Yeah, but..."? Trace it back to its origin. Who told you that? Where did those ideas come from? Are they rooted in Love or passed down from someone else's discomfort?

Privilege is when I get to change the narrative because the truth offends me.

Privilege is when I demand an account of all the "productive" ways you've shown up for injustice when I'm rankled by the way you peacefully protest injustice.

Privilege is when I value my opinion above seeking to understand what led to your actions.

Misinformed outrage at peaceful resistance destroys the bridge of forgiveness and reconciliation. How do we ever get to the other side if we do not humble ourselves to hear a reality that expresses concerns and fears different from our own?

Erasure and assimilation are no longer acceptable solutions to long-held problems.

Did we really get to the point that we can't say "Black Lives Matter" because "I don't agree with all the tenets of the movement"?

I mean, I don't agree with every facet of America as an institution either, but it's never stopped me from pledging allegiance to the flag or singing the national anthem.

How sanctimonious of us to be so in our feels....

Let's stop being personally offended long enough to address the collective systemic issues that racism and inequity have perpetuated in society.

Yielding power

scares most people into clutching their privileged pearls.

The ego never wants to concede.

Neither does authentic power want to be a master.

Authentic power welcomes mutuality.

You're powerful and I'm powerful.

We are vast,

Progress is the recognition and acceptance of authentic power without fear of dominance or subjugation.

Money over humanity

Money over decency

Money over ecology

Money over the common good

The underbelly of capitalism: greed + fear of not having enough

is the thread

that unravels peace and all good things.

It's imperative to know that people are wounded. They are hurting—whether we understand it or agree with it.

It's imperative to know that a divide *does* exist. No one is saying you created the divide.

It's equally imperative that we only own what's ours to own. Standing in solidarity with the hurting, with the marginalized, is Christlike. How we choose to do that is very personal.

But again, my heart compels you—let's do the work of healing.

Yes, it might be a little uncomfortable, allowing someone to be in pain, not knowing exactly what to do or what to say. We're fixers, after all. We want to hurry up and smooth things over so everyone goes back to being happy pretenders again.

No, let's not.

There's a huge invitation to Love across the chasm.

May our action lead to compassion and our compassion to action.

I'm reminded of a story I once heard.

One day, a little girl ran home crying. In much distress, she cried, "Oh, Mom!"

With outstretched arms, her mom embraced her. She held the girl, allowed her to cry. While the mom consoled the girl, she knew something the daughter, in her pain, could not yet know. She knew it would eventually get better—maybe not now, while the pain was still raw, but the mom had walked this way before, and, with that knowing, she held the girl, absorbing her daughter's pain, extending to the girl her peace, exchanging in real time peace for pain, as only a Love-bearer can do.

So, let's be clear. No one is saying racism, fear, or hate is new. I am saying they are being exposed. And now that they are resurfacing, it's a beautiful invitation for those of us who carry Love to cast aside the tendency to justify or defend and wholeheartedly partner with Divine Love.

Let's embrace those who might need it and hand them our peace. Let's not be too quick to rush the healing. The last thing we need is to push the agony beneath the surface again with platitudes that placate our discomfort with others' pain.

As close as the moon is to the earth, in this moment, let's be that close to our brothers and sisters in their pain. You're welcome to make this about politics. It's certainly applicable, but the depth of the truth is far greater than any system.

My ancestors

survived the middle passage,

came to a distant shore, hearing a language they did not speak,

expected to follow orders, get in line, and walk miles in shackles to places unknown:

to till someone else's land,

to make someone else rich,

to establish generational wealth and ease for someone else's family—

and yet they called my ancestors

stupid

lazy

unintelligent.

Heads bloodied but unbowed,

my ancestors learned a new language on their own.

With no Rosetta Stone,

they learned the master's ways:

his ire,

his rhythm,

and how to stay alive—

and they did.

They survived

plantations

rape, mutilations, branding, starvation

chain gangs

sharecropping

lynching

the Jim Crow South—

even the hatred and racism that followed the trail of promise north on the Great Migration.

This is the people from whom I hail:

survivors

learners

people skilled in assessment

intuitive people

healers

workers.

Head upon my pillow,

I think of how shady people have been.

I remember all the enslavers, slave runners, slave patrols, southern sheriffs, and klansmen—every dastardly misdeed

done with smiles;

cowlicks, eyes twinkling with merriment at getting away with

mischief, wrongdoing;

smug, haughty,

feeling themselves, their rightness.

Then, I think again of my ancestors.

I think of how we were taught to work:

Put our heads down.

Stay out of trouble.

Do what you need

to make it through the day.

Survive.

Stay low. Stay quiet. Don't make trouble...

and I think of a wave,

the agitation required in the ocean floor to stir its formation,

gathering strength,

building to a crescendo,

cascading over,

cleansing,

sweeping with it all the murky debris.

May the wave of fortitude it took for us to survive,

to reach this point in history,

crash upon our memory

like a resounding gong:

Remember who you are.

Remember from whence you hail.

We have been forged in the fire

and we have survived.

Too many Black women grow up in a world of Judy Garland, Marilyn Monroe, Dolly Parton, Brooke Shields, the Kardashians, and the list goes on and on.

A world with dolls or books that portray our reality has not always been accessible or affordable. A world of hierarchal colorism meant the lighter you were, the better you were because the closer to white you were.

In 2019, Miss Tennessee, Miss USA, Miss Teen USA, Miss America, and Miss Universe were all Black. It may seem small, these crowns, these queens, these stunning feats. But know that to Black women everywhere, these women are mirrors—mirrors of our beauty, mirrors of our intelligence, mirrors of our poise, mirrors of our leadership, mirrors of our existence and our being—to every little Black girl looking in the mirror, trying to figure out exactly who is staring back at her. Who looks like her? Where is her place in the world? The spotlight is shining on these examples, and we applaud them all.

And if you think for a second this is a Black/white thing, it isn't. I watched my friend's daughter's eyes light up at a parade when a float of Latina pageant winners, adorned in their gowns and crowns, rolled by. The beautiful little girl, who happens to be Puerto Rican and Asian, turned to her mom with innocent wonder. It swelled my heart to see the awe in her eyes. But it also confirms that every culture needs mirrors.

Some may even wonder, "What's the big deal about having women of color win national beauty pageants?" For far too long, only one culture has dominated the reflection and image of our America.

Today, I invite you to celebrate with us as more diverse mirrors are offered to a generation in dire need of seeing themselves.

And I'd love to offer my friend Jen's wise words: "A world with no mirrors, a place inside and out where we barely recognize the angle of light or the shape of things around us and in us, is literally terrifying. And it's not because we're not trying hard or because there is no beauty…it is because there is no recognition. And it's scary."

Mirrors—we need them.

"You may write me down in history with your bitter, twisted lies."[10]

Chattel, you call me:

Less than human you see me

as you slink between my thighs.

You beat our men

with braided cords,

rape our women

while calling them whores.

Monstrous acts of pain

wreaking havoc and destruction.

10. Maya Angelou, "Still I Rise," *Phenomenal Woman: Four Poems Celebrating Women* (New York: Random House, 1995), 7.

Maddening policies to hide your obsession

with superiority,

with dominance.

You say you love but your actions breed dissonance.

Friend of what stranger?

Brother to what foreigner?

The tired at our borders have no place to lay their heads.

Ears deaf to pleas of mercy.

Bloodied hands raised in worship

to white Jesus, Zeus's God,

the "greatness" of America

threaded in whip lashes across the backs of generations…

How easy the master's grandsons remember the master's tools.

Morality cannot be legislated, but behavior can be regulated.
Judicial decrees may not change the heart, but they can restrain
the heartless.
—Martin Luther King Jr.[11]

Behavior modification has failed us—or at least that's what I believe.

My friend Trevor Galpin always says, "When the heart is changed, we will automatically be different because your heart is who you are."

I believe that.

I know that to be true of my own becoming.

But I also know the world does not have time for every evil person's heart to be changed of their own accord before legislation changes to protect the most marginalized person in our midst.

And while I want to lean in to Love for a nondual understanding of the dance between legislating the collective and inner transformation, sometimes I feel like Paul the apostle as my heart breaks for our society.

O, foolish Americans. Who has bewitched you?

Do you not know that the push and pull you feel is intentional?

---

11. "Martin Luther King Jr., April 27, 1965," Communication Studies Department, UCLA, *YouTube*, www.youtube.com/watch?v=ny6qP0rb_Ag.

Do you not understand this fear was harnessed?

The intent of its power is to drive a wedge between us.

It is within the heart that all wars are won: the heart, the seat of our authentic power.

Lives are overrun by power—the need for it, the certainty of it, the subjugation of it, to lord over another and dominate.

And so we fight. We wrestle.

We get pulled into the melee of ego's power struggle.

Stop. Pause. Listen.

Listen to the sound of your own heart.

And then, listen to the sound of another.

"What is in your heart you need me to hear?" Offer reciprocity instead of defense.

We have forgotten our beauty, our strength, and our resiliency, opting instead to discount, deny, and overlook the pain we've wrought on one another. We can no longer afford for people to modify their behavior without addressing the condition of their heart.

We can't go forward without a reckoning of the past. The unsanitized truth must be given space to breathe. Let the secrets hit the air.

"How dare you share that with the world?" "How dare you paint America in such light? She bathed you, fed you, kept you warm at night. You should be grateful for all she's done."

I know...I know the truth is painful to bear full-on. It's why we've always told it slant,[12] whitewashed it, prettied it up.

But now, now is the time to bear it, to tell it, and to not ridicule others in their revealing.

May we have the courage to open our minds, our hearts, our hands. May the spell be broken, and may we come to ourselves.

---

12. See Emily Dickinson's "Tell all the truth but tell it slant," www. poetryfoundation.org/poems/56824/tell-all-the-truth-but-tell-it-slant-1263.

A beautiful world is waiting, but we cannot get there the same way we reached and developed these shores.

Be encouraged. *"Love never fails."*[13]

Sometimes things have to break open and fall apart in order to come together. Don't turn from the discomfort. Don't hide from the wrestle.

I can't help but think of Mamie Till's decision to allow her son's murdered and mutilated body to lie in an open casket for public viewing, so people could see the atrocity of not only what happens to Black men and women, but the level of vile hate one would have to possess to brutally, ritually, mindfully maim another without remorse.

Emmett Till's body was a mirror for society.

But it was Mamie Till's brave decision to lay the truth bare that invited us in to see ourselves.

And here we are again, needing to see ourselves.

Don't run.

Stand. Relax your shoulders. Soften your belly.

Eyes wide open.

Breathe deep and decide you're here for this.

Let's all be here for this.

---

13. First Corinthians 13:8.

"Mack, for you to forgive this man is for you to release him to me and allow me to redeem him."

"Redeem him?" Again Mack felt the fire of anger and hurt. "I don't want you to redeem him! I want you to hurt him, to punish him, to put him in hell..." His voice trailed off.

Papa waited patiently for the emotions to ease.

"I'm stuck, Papa. I can't just forget what he did, can I?" Mack implored.

"Forgiveness is not about forgetting, Mack. It is about letting go of another person's throat."

"But I thought you forget our sins."

"Mack, I am God. I forget nothing. I know everything. So forgetting for me is the choice to limit myself. Son"—Papa's voice got quiet and Mack looked up at him, directly into his deep brown eyes—"because of Jesus, there is now no law demanding that I bring your sins back to mind. They are gone when it comes to you and me, and they run no interference in our relationship."

"But this man..."

"But he too is my son. I want to redeem him."[14]

Justice!" the heart screams. "Vengeance. Let them feel what I feel. Show them what it's like to live in fear, to lose, to suffer, to grieve."

14. William Paul Young, *The Shack: Where Tragedy Confronts Eternity* (Newbury Park, CA: Windblown Media, 2007).

...and my heart breaks into a thousand tiny pieces. For doing so changes nothing.

We keep holding society by the throat while our internal world is in an uproar—angry, mad. Using anger to address anger only produces more anger. And it's so easy to get caught up in the energy of its tidal wave. Such is the surge of its power source.

Still, there is Love, gently encouraging us to feel what we feel and let go.

With eyes full of love and a heart wide open in sympathy and understanding, there is Love saying to us all, "But they are also my children. Would you have me do to them what I would never do to the least of these?"

May it never be so.

"For God so loved the world."[15]

When I learned that my "tribe" was the whole of humanity and not a select circle of a few hundred people where we all parroted the same Christianese, my heart was reborn in love to a greater perspective, one that doesn't have to choose Israel over Palestine, my race over another, women over men, conservative over liberal.

It's a perspective that destroys hierarchies and enlarges my view of the circle of life.

The Beloved calls us all to this perspective of love.

This perspective is free from intimidation, insecurity, fear, and worry of what others perceive.

It's not easily threatened and isn't territorial.

It's a welcoming perspective that excludes no one nor forces someone to think like me.

In this holistic view of acceptance, my heart is no longer pitted against or fragmented. My heart has been made whole.

---

15. John 3:16.

I believe in people. I believe in freedom.

I believe in choice, even if it's sometimes merely an illusion.

I believe in Divine Love, who is Being.

I believe love is love.

I believe in the scent of newborn babes with freshly washed hair smelling of Johnson's baby oil.

I believe in the smell of freshly cut grass, deep green from chlorophyll.

I believe in rum and Coke, preferably from Haiti or Jamaica.

I believe in the shared table, complete with half-filled wine glasses and food for sustenance.

I believe in the power of laughter and an uncoerced smile.

I believe in good, frequent, consented lovemaking between partners and a good breeze that ushers peace into the atmosphere.

I believe in Spirit as Source Energy, the alignment of frequency that exists and thrums through all creation—rock, plant, animal, people, ecosystems, solar system—leading us into all Truth.

I believe in the universality of the Cosmic Christ and union with the Divine.

What I can't believe is that in my lifetime, a man lost the ability to play a professional sport because he took a knee for something he believed in and would not cower, even in the face of sacrificing his economic livelihood.

There is one race—the human race, which exists in varying shades of color.

I imagine people of that one race, the human race, spreading from Africa across the earth, sharing distinctive cultures (*ethnos*) and forming ethnic groups and tribes.

I imagine the closer to the equator that members of the human race were and the longer the sun remained in the sky, the darker their shade of skin. The farther away from the sun, the paler the shades of skin.

I write "imagine" because I was not there in the beginning, and I am no scientist or expert on melanin or pigmentation.

Thus, I imagine this to be true of our origin until one somebody somewhere, or a group of somebodies somewhere, decided to attach identity and value to the color of skin.

Labels created,

race constructed and measured, creating levels of import for the ego.

White became right.

Dark became bad, evil, and everything malevolent.

Race is a false classification created to give some among the human race a sense of power and to legitimize their dominance over other members of the human race.

Some members of the human race even participated in "white passing" to benefit from the privileges offered to those who, as a result of the legitimation of race classification, exerted superiority and dominance. That's how deeply humanity bought into this construct when it was introduced in Jacques de Brézé's 1481 poem "The Hunt" and expanded over the next century to animalize African people.

May we imagine a new truth about our origin: We are from the same Source. May we hold our oneness without weaponizing the truth to bypass the issues of systemic oppression, which has led to marginalization of people of color.

We are one race, the human race.

And since Jean Nicot's construction of race appeared in the dictionary in 1606, nothing but subjugation, domination, oppression, isolation, marginalization, etc. has come from the idea...that is, unless you benefit from the privilege of being at the top of the "racial" caste system.

Performative expressions feel good, and we can float them around to show how we all can get along: quick fixes to move beyond our internal discomfort. But just beyond outward kumbaya expressions that give the appearance of unity is the momentum to change systemic oppression and right injustice.

This is about social activism: Disrupting the system. Changing the system.

Who are the most marginalized persons or people groups in your local area, community, state, region, and nation? What legislation and civic changes need to be addressed to ensure they are empowered to live?

But first things first. First, we acknowledge that the system is what it is. Be honest about humanity's failings and its abuse of power.

The system was built for the dominant culture to thrive and everyone else to be subservient. The system was given legitimacy by perpetuating the idea of a savior, and in order for the savior to succeed, he needs destitute people in dire straits to save.

Every hero needs a victim afraid of a villain. The system created a narrative that white men were the heroes, white women were the victims, and Blacks and Natives were the villains.

If you don't believe me, watch *Tarzan* (and hundreds of other tired Hollywood movies built on this triangle).

The system perpetuates this mindset, which is why most of our congressional leaders, governors, and presidents are old white men who position themselves as saviors of others. "Look at all I've done for you..."

Even our subconscious/unconscious biases are conditioned by the system.

We think women need to be protected, not lead a nation. Ask Elizabeth Warren, Hillary Clinton, and Stacey Abrams.

For eight years, a Black man served in the highest office and every day, from the beginning of his campaign, he was villainized, particularly by our forty-fifth president, who launched his birther smear campaign and dogged his predecessor almost constantly on Twitter.

Poverty, inferiority, and suspicion are all tools of the system to help the hero and the victim easily identify who will be scapegoated as their villain.

In order to imagine a new way forward, we will first have to admit and accept that things were meant to be the way they are.

Acceptance brings me to a choice. And choice is our most sacred act.

We can accept that the system is the way it is, dig our heels in, put our head in the sand, not vote, sit this one out, and resign ourselves to fatalism, *or* we can accept that the system is the way it is, but it doesn't have to stay this way.

Think about it.

What do you need to acknowledge? What do you need to accept? What do you need to reimagine?

What will you do with the power of your choice?

There's no such thing as a nonracist. Either you are destroying this and looking to dismantle this thing that currently exists, and you're working towards it and you're working towards developing culture around it, or you're either devout or complicit. And so, for me, when white people say these things that they think are supportive because they speak a different language than I do, a different embodied language, a different verbal language, what they're actually telling me is, "You are not safe."[16]
—Resmaa Menakem in a conversation
with Robin Diangelo and Krista Tippett

Every time I see a friend post something to defend or justify the harmful actions of another,

my insides flutter and I feel like I could vomit.

16. Resmaa Menakem, "Interview with Krista Tippett and Robin DiAngelo," *On Being with Krista Tippett*, podcast audio, July 9, 2020, onbeing.org/programs/robin-diangelo-and-resmaa-menakem-towards-a-framework-for-repair.

The chasm of our divide seems great.

What people who are hurting want and need most is someone to bear witness to their pain.

Right or wrong, can you stand with me in solidarity and say, "I see you. I hear you. I'm with you"?

Hurting people don't give a rat's behind about your defense or justification.

Their momentary cry is, "I'm in pain. This is hurting me. Can't you see that? For one moment, I'm asking you to put aside your rationalism, your need to justify, your need to defend, and hear my heart."

There's a sigh of relief in being heard, in being known.

Please, friends, before you post something, take a moment and ask yourself:

Am I posting this to defend my position?

Am I hearing the heart cry of those in pain when

I share this, or will this post once again drown out

their plea to be heard?

What the world needs is for us to move toward effective dialogue that's rooted in mutuality, love, and understanding.

This is gonna take a lot more than holding hands in church on Sunday and singing kumbaya. Begin by managing what you can with the intentionality of reconciliation and equality.

Love yields, but remains engaged.

I wonder if we miss the heart of Love when we talk about "the melting pot" and "not seeing color."

Imagine examining the work of Cezanne, Rembrandt, Van Gogh, or Monet and saying, "I only see a blank canvas. They all look the same."

To say we're a melting pot implies a lack of individuality.

To say we see no color implies invisibility.

Great Creator was so intentional when creating each one of us, taking thought to the color of our skin, the color of our eyes and our hair, our ethnicity, our nationality.

Everything about us displays the Holy Three's brilliancy as a Master Artist and screams love and intentionality.

Instead of melting or not seeing, let's celebrate each other's uniqueness and beauty.

Look with your eyes and enjoy the tapestry the Beloved created, called the human race.

We are brilliant. We are beautiful. We are each called to display Love's glory.

Look someone in the eyes today and, with your love turned full on, say, "I see you. I see everything about you, and it's beautiful. Created in the image and likeness of Divine Love, you are glory on display."

*In times of despair, agreement isn't necessary. Safety is.
All things considered, what is the most loving thing I can do
to ensure the safety of this person's welfare?*

If I have the mindset that people in crisis are entitled and are only looking for a handout— "They want everything done for them."—or even a hand up, that mindset permeates my belief system, even the way I govern.

And if I feel someone doesn't deserve help because they are already indebted and fiscally irresponsible—"They already owe a massive debt."—and have no clear plan to repay my assistance, then I'm going to be slow in my desire to lend aid and compassion to people I feel are undeserving of help.

But that's the thing about labels and aliases: Once we saddle people with judgments like "lazy" or "entitled," once we decide who we should or shouldn't help based on our opinion of their lifestyle and their situation, we remove our hearts from a compassionate response.

Yet *"mercy triumphs over judgment."*[17]

May love and light flood places in despair with clean water, cash, food, fuel, and able-bodied workers to rebuild roads and repair infrastructure.

May our true colors of love and compassion shine above our politics.

May we, the people, see the people.

May we, the people, be the people.

---

17. James 2:13.

I have a friend who read Austin Channing Brown's *I'm Still Here: Black Dignity in a World Made for Whiteness* because I mentioned in passing this was the book about race and the "Kingdom" that I could have written, would have written, and now no longer need to write because Austin pretty much said everything I would have said. My friend read the book because I said this book encapsulates 89 to 90 percent of my life. Like, close my eyes and insert my name and a few life situations, and we almost have the same thing. And because my friend always desires to know me in richer, deeper ways, she read the book so we could talk about it in depth.

I love my friend. We laugh together, we eat together, we drink wine together. We do lots of fun things together. But if fun is all we can ever do in our friendship when larger, prevalent, hurtful, damning, life-changing issues and policies are at play in the world—in *my* world—that might give me pause.

I never asked my friend to read Austin's book. I never even knew she took what I said about the book, that "fun" day on our walk in the gardens, and tucked it away in her heart. I've never asked my friend to have one conversation with me about race or to show up in things that matter to me, but somehow, she always does. Always.

When I preach, she drives an hour and a half one way to sit in the back row and be there for me. When my kids have things, she's there or she's sending a card or a Venmo. She remembers birthdays and details. She supports my other friend's work because my other friend matters to me. My friend asks questions. She listens. And I hope I am one ounce of a friend in reciprocity to her that she is to me.

This thing in our world, in our America *and* globally (because don't think for a minute we're the only ones dealing with this stuff)—this place of racial tension, gender tension, socioeconomic tension, religious tension—is going to require some talking about it. It's going to require some uneasy, uncomfortable moments of conversation that are highly opinionated because what is our egoic self if not our opinion? And since this is the level in which this conversation is taking place, it's very likely that these conversations won't be fun, but it doesn't mean the conversation isn't necessary.

Especially if you have a heart to know and understand from a position that is not your own, which I think is key.

Can I recognize that someone else may have a different opinion, a different experience, a different perspective? Am I interested enough in that person to want to take the time to know it, to hear it, to attempt to understand it, even on a small, microscopic level?

Are people worth the exchange?

My friend's actions tell me all the time that I'm worth the exchange.

And I want that to be said of me, that when people leave my presence, whether we've been there for fun stuff or opinionated stuff or hard stuff or wine, I want them to walk away feeling like I showed up and created space for them to do the same.

In what ways do your friends say, "You're worth it"?

How are you showing up and creating space for others to be?

All too often, "Christianity" in white spaces is synonymous with politeness.

Black people learn to go along to get along. They bite their tongue and clamp down on their rebuttals rather than ruffle feathers, make noise, or share their piece. They're opting to keep a false sense of peace rather than trouble the waters of kumbaya.

Ask most white pastors of multiethnic churches, and they are likely to tell you race isn't an issue in their church. They've transcended

Ask most of the Black congregants, out of the white pastor's presence, and they are likely to suggest a different narrative—one where they chose to say nothing about certain issues rather than rock the boat. One where they placed the comfortability of a white church member over their own discomfort rather than have to go through the struggle of finding another place to worship. Ask about how many microaggressions they've had to overlook or discount or write off just to rationalize in their minds attending church in a so-called "peaceable" kingdom.

Lord, in your mercy...

May we hear the voices of the oppressed,

the voices of the marginalized.

May we be truth-tellers and love-bearers and people

who will honor the sacredness of humanity above

greed and polarization.

May we be honest about the ways we've been

complicit in the suffering and degradation of others

without merely washing our hands and leaving

people to figure it out for themselves.

We, in America, did that with the Emancipation Proclamation, and we see how well that worked out for too many of us.

Would that we could be people who learn from our past instead of continually repeating it.

*"Make them aware. Don't minimize it to make
people comfortable.
Don't ignore it and move from it. Make people aware."*

Dualism and dichotomy of extremes splits our interconnectedness.

In fact, I'd wager that "inter-" is not a prefix America is yet ready for.

We're still struggling to navigate the tension of differences, and as long as the fabric of trust remains eroded between different versions of America, I will not believe that you have my best interest at heart.

"I will protect what's mine at the expense of what's yours" is not loving your neighbor as yourself.

At some point, America will have to:

- Acknowledge the harm.

- Repair trust.

- Move toward liberty (freedom for all, not just the rich, the powerful, and the unborn).

Until we are ready to do that, terror and theory will remain tactics of tyranny—tactics to divide us, keep us separated from one another.

From beyond the veil, the casualties of tyranny, martyrs to police brutality beseech us to acknowledge our missed opportunities to collectively own the loss and damage to life as we thought we knew it.

The gift of disruption is its invitation to begin again—to reorder.

In the words of a dear friend, "The only way forward is toward."

Does the story you tell yourself center around protecting privilege and the illusion of safety, hoarding dollars and capital gains? Or is it aimed toward people, toward a more equitable, inclusive version of what could be?

This is not simple. Neither is the solution a quick, easy fix. We cannot get there without acknowledging the layers and complexity of our story. There is nuance and backstory, a meandering path of violence and love, greed and generosity, perseverance and cheating—the good and bad of all humanity bound together in its telling.

This telling requires us to:

- Acknowledge how we have missed the mark, how the way of our being has not aligned with what we say is the truth of our being.

- Lament the wrongs, the atrocities, and the decisions to allow fear to pimp us into choosing self-protection and scarcity over shared abundance and generosity.

- Move toward one another in love.

This is the invitation before us. Will we attend its opportunity or discard it as mere rubbish?

I have the great fortune of being a Felicia. I love my name. It means happy, joyful, felicity, bliss. But some asinine movie flippantly turned my beautiful name into a dis, and every time people wield that phrase (even as a joke), I feel the dismissal like a punch in the gut.

Maybe I'm a bit too sensitive? Who knows.

The feeling is hard to explain if you're not a person who feels deeply or your name isn't Felicia.

But I will say this: That feeling, that dismissal, is exactly what it feels like when people write or say, "All lives matter."

Cancer matters.

Diabetes matters.

All diseases matter,

but the one most afflicting the health of our nation is racism.

All houses are important.

All houses hold history, people, belongings, culture, memories.

But if your house is the one on fire with a four-alarm bell to the fire department at this specific time,

your house matters.

And while that takes nothing away from the other houses of importance surrounding the burning house, right now, my dear sisters and brothers, "The roof is on fire."

And that good ole refrain, "All lives matter," might as well be the bass line at the club: "We don't need no water—let the…"[18]

18. Rock Master Scott & The Dynamic Three, "The Roof Is on Fire," Reality Records, 1985.

Some people are being killed because of their humanity—the color of their skin.

Some people are being killed because they opted to work in a vocation that calls them to put their life on the line.

Whether death by police brutality—fear, dehumanization, power trip—or death as a result of career choice, the common denominator remains the same: Some people are being killed.

The volleying of violence, the need to rank one senseless death over another, is what happens when we cling to an us-versus-them mentality.

Our fight should never lead to more senseless killing or purposeless incarceration.

I stand with Love in the center, holding the hearts of my people—our anger, our frustration, our grief, our bone-weary tiredness. I hold the pain, the tears, the exhaustion. I hold our fear. I hold that place in the wounded soul that wants to strike back and seek revenge.

And, for a moment, with Love, I'm just letting it all be: not trying to fix it, not trying to bless it or send it away, but holding it, acknowledging it, just as Love did when the Holy Three bore our grief and sickness.

And I hold the hearts of the law enforcement officers (LEOs), people with whom I can't readily identify, for I've not spent any time walking in their life, but Love has.

So I stand with Love, holding their hearts, their pain, and their frustration with being misunderstood and mistrusted—whether justified or not. I hold the fear they carry for their lives.

In the center, Love breaks down the wall of us versus them. In the center, the accusations of the evil one that whisper, *"Crucify him"*[19] in the ears of the other are silenced by peace.

To the LEOs who have lost their lives...to the families of the men and women who have brutally lost their lives...for you, for the others, for all the fallen who are a testament in death that violence is not the answer, we seek peaceful resolutions—but not in the halls of the White House or through mandated behavior modification that creates a false image of change.

No, we seek answers and resolutions that first begin with an inner transformation of our own hearts and then continue through civic engagement rooted in love.

I mourn for our fallen sons, and I mourn for the fallen LEOs. No one deserves to die senselessly. It doesn't have to be either/or, us versus them. We can choose to stand with Love in the circle of Life.

I'm determined to be a voice of peace. I will not fight. I will not boycott. (This is not to say there isn't a place for fighting or boycotting, or that neither is effective. This is to say what I will do and what I won't do. I am speaking as me, for me only.)

I will not force from you something you don't choose to freely give.

I demand nothing of you, for demands and force have not worked out well for any of us.

In love, I ask you to choose unity because you want to, not because you have to.

There is a place in love for people to coexist without fear. Choose love.

---

19. Luke 23:21.

Power is as intoxicating as a heroin trip.

White power.

Black power.

Religious power.

Political power.

Patriarchal power.

Absolute power corrupts absolutely.

The story of separation perpetuates Killmongers[20] who desire anarchy and annihilation over peace and coexistence.

---

20. N'Jadaka/Erik "Killmonger" Stevens is the name of a character in the Marvel Comics superhero film *Black Panther*, directed by Ryan Coogler (2018; Walt Disney Studios Motion Pictures).

*I always wonder if the same people hop in the inboxes of Black
male pastors who constantly preach messages that dehumanize
Black women. Do they have this same amount of smoke for
White clergy and religious thinkers who preach anti-Blackness
and white supremacy as if it were the gospel of Jesus Christ? Or
do we just reserve this kind of venom and gaslighting for the
Black women we can no longer control and regulate? Does the
notion of a free Black woman frighten you more than misogy-
nistic Black men and racist White people? Black people, Black
women especially, have embraced spiritual fluidity for centuries.
This ain't new; it is home. And, though it may not be how you
choose to live into your faith, it doesn't make it demonic or mean
that the Black women who embrace this are less holy than you.*
—Candice Benbow

I didn't even know spiritual fluidity was a thing, but I'd like to offer
us some things to consider, like how enslavers used Christianity to
colonize their chattel slavery and how the residual effects of that have
tarnished interpretations of the gospel for centuries.

I didn't even realize Augustine was African until a few months
ago. Much less Origen.

Completely stripped of his Middle Eastern/North African fea-
tures, the idea of a pale-faced, blue-eyed, stringy-brown-haired Jesus
lends itself to conditioning the mind to believe all of his disciples and
subsequent theologians also looked the same.

At some point, we have to stop and ask ourselves, "Is this intentional?" How has demonizing every other religion and declaring yours the "only" way played into and supported ideals of superiority and supremacy?

Is the answer to swing the system the other way, so that all positions of power are held by people of color while being supported by the finances of whites, or is there a third way that isn't just a swing of positional power?

While this may never happen in our day, what is the win for equality and humanization that moves us beyond a volleying of who's in control and who has the power? What is the third way to racial conciliation that isn't power driven: "white power" or "Black power"?

Two things are at play for me...

First, **"AND"**—I totally believe that ontologically, we are one human race AND because I believe that God is so intentional, I am remiss to deny the particularities of our biodiversity among humans, plants, fish, animals, flowers, etc.

If I am to believe in the creative ingenuity of our Creator, I feel like if God wanted us all to be homogeneous, we would have been. But we aren't.

And I wonder if that's not the invitation of grace: that we learn to hold the tension of ontological oneness while relationally weaving the particularities of our diversity into a beautiful tapestry as we do the work of navigating this messy, beautiful, complex, divine journey we call life.

I don't want a singular humanity at the expense of our diversity. I want both.

It feels to me as if the Trinity and our known ecosystems invite us into that.

Secondly, I don't think we achieve ontological oneness by erasing our history, the hard and the good of it, or our culture. We can't bypass our way to harmony.

But if we could admit that this is complicated and allow space for each one of us to hear "the sound of the genuine,"[21] to use Howard Thurman's words, as we attune ourselves to love through the composition of life's complexity, we'll produce music together.

History then serves as borders for the tapestry we are weaving together.

I keep thinking of Jesus and how he came to fulfill the law, not negate it. He didn't erase the law or deny the law existed, and while he was a little stern with the Pharisees, I believe he offered us a Way of Love that was a correction to their failures and missteps.

Did this rub some people the wrong way? Absolutely.

They took offense to him not honoring and keeping the law in the same regard. They were not interested in his reform or ideas about change. Maybe Jesus was *too spiritually fluid* for their taste.

Past generations of African-Americans were more silent about disparities and inequities, largely because of the lynchings that happened during the Jim Crow era. Black America went from boisterous leaders like Fannie Lou Hamer, Frederick Douglass, W.E.B. Du Bois, James Baldwin, and others to grandmothers teaching their children to keep their heads down, shrink, and stay silent. Do what you need to survive. Or you were taught to pursue education to assimilate. Education was god for Blacks because, other than being a preacher, education was the only possible way out of inequitable situations of despair.

Even this was a long-held debate in the Black community. Booker T. Washington argued that Blacks should continue to work the land. He believed agriculture and self-sufficiency were key to empowerment.

Du Bois argued for education and the talented tenth, that reputable Blacks should strive to become educated, to assimilate into

21. Howard Thurman, "The Sound of the Genuine," Spelman College Commencement Speech, May 4, 1980.

mainstream lifestyles. He leaned more toward the politics of respectability—until he didn't.

This tension between "separate but equal," for which Washington and later the Black Panthers advocated, and assimilation, favored by Du Bois, is still in some ways being played out culturally in the forceful voices that we hear today.

And sadly, some of the younger generation (and quite possibly boomers as well) are trying to use *power over* in the same way power over has been used against them. I don't believe a hard swing in a direction opposite of white supremacy is what Love is inviting us into.

What I'm interested in is how we hold our ontological oneness *and* the particularities of our diversity with deep regard, *and* tell the truth, *and* be carriers of Love, *and* celebrate our sameness and our differences without diminishing anyone in the process.

&

TEND THE WOUND

On their journey, Jesus came into a village. There was a woman there named Martha, who welcomed him. She had a sister named Mary, who sat at the master's feet and listened to his teaching. Martha was frantic with all the work in the kitchen. "Master," she said, coming in to where they were, "don't you care that my sister has left me to do the work all by myself? Tell her to give me a hand!" "Martha, Martha," he replied, "you are fretting and fussing about so many things. Only one thing matters. Mary has chosen the best part, and it's not going to be taken away from her."
—Luke 10:38–42 NTE

Even though Jesus does not specifically name what Mary chose, if you're like me, you've probably heard dozens, if not hundreds, of sermons on what Mary chose. And it is not my goal to add yet another treatise on Mary. I actually want to focus on Martha, but before I do…

Mary.

Ponder with me the words of Jesus: *"Only one thing matters. Mary has chosen the best part."*

What if the best part was an invitation to wholeness, an invitation for Mary to be true to herself? An invitation that Mary fully and completely owned: This is who I am—I am a disciple of Jesus. This is where I want to be—I want to sit at his feet and learn. This is the *yes* I'm living into in this moment.

This is my holy sacrament—to fully and consciously participate with self-emptying Love in this present moment.

What does choosing the best part look like for you? Could it be—as Paul Young, *New York Times* best-selling author of *The Shack* encourages—living in the grace of this one day?

And if that looks like sitting at the feet of Jesus, soaking in his teaching and wisdom, sit. If that looks like cooking and serving, cook. Serve. If that looks like academic rigor for you, study. If it looks like solitude for you, meditate.

"Mary has chosen the best part," or *the good portion.* She knows what she has said yes to in this moment, and her yes is hers alone. She's owning what she has chosen, what she holds most precious in the moment. She's not projecting it or trying to force it on another. She's not demanding her sister, or anyone else, take up the causes she's passionate about or do the same things she does. She's chosen the best part—she's given her full attention to this moment she's said yes to *and* she's not trying to pull her sister out of conscious participation with what she's said yes to.

I am, may you be.[22]

And then, there's Martha.

I wonder. What judgment did Martha make? What did Martha assume about Mary, about Jesus? What lie did she believe? What socialized constructs and cultural practices had she normalized and bought into? What assumptions, traditions, and expectations shaped Martha's role and the way she moved and ordered her existence?

Martha welcomed Jesus. She was frantic with the work in the kitchen.

---

22. cf. Beatrice Bruteau, *Holy Thursday Revolution* (Maryknoll, NY: Orbis, 2005), 71.

Whether this story is literal, metaphorical, allegorical, or per-haps a multilayered, complex mix of all three, I'll leave that for theo-logians and those scholars who are trained for that discourse. I always like to be clear that I'm neither. I'm just curious about what Love is inviting me to see.

And while the historical cultural context of this story certainly is important, I'd like to make a comparative leap through the lens of my own lived experience and invite us to think about:

+ What assumptions we make with the little we are given of the exchange in this text.

+ What assumptions I'm making as I share my thoughts with you.

What did Jesus observe? Seeing Mary at his feet; seeing the same Martha who had welcomed him now rushing in, anxious and dis-turbed about many things; what was it like for Jesus to observe this interplay?

I think a lot about systems, people groups, and relational dynamics.

What I see, what I'd like to see, what moves me, and what grieves me, I think about how rigid we can be in what we think is right and how our sense of certainty doesn't often leave room for people trying to find their way, their own language. How, in an effort to right the sinking ship of individualism or move too quickly past the discomfort of current events playing out in our day-to-day, we can paint the col-lective in such a broad stroke that we lose the distinction and beauty of particularity.

I think about how it scares us when others deviate from our *shoulds* and then what we do with our own fear, the demands we make, and the things we say. And, over and over again, I keep bump-ing into this line from *The Shack*: "I suppose since most of our hurts come through relationships, so will our healing."[23]

---

23. Young, *The Shack*.

But I'm not certain we can get to healing without acknowledging our hurts. And as I think about all the things, I wonder if we can adequately articulate what we need to heal. Have we sat long enough with ourselves and with Spirit to articulate what is the real cry of our heart in the racial discord and political divide of our day?

If love is the structure in which freedom is governed, then how do we live freely with those who oppose or care less about our existence and full humanity? How do we live and move and have our being in concert with others among the dissonance and clashes?

Martha had an idea of what needed to be done and set about doing it. Inside of the execution of that idea, there was never a moment in her mind's eye where Mary's assistance was not included in her plan. Martha assumed her sister would take her proper, *rightful* place in serving their honored guest and his companions. Women were, and still are in most settings, expected to fulfill these duties.

If I could pull out for emphasis some words from what I've written: Martha had an idea; she had created a narrative or picture, imagined how this would go.

She built a plan around the story she told herself, which included how others (namely, Mary and Jesus) should operate in given roles to get to the outcome she desired.

Imagined. Assumed. Expected.

And what happened when things didn't go as she imagined? Did she spiral into disappointment, frustration? Did she feel abandoned by Mary? Did she get mad at her, at Jesus?

Expectations tie us to outcomes. Expectations are often disappointments waiting to happen because people are one variable that we cannot control, even though it never stops us from trying.

When facing disappointment over what we imagined, assumed, and expected, how do we posture ourselves in relationship to be mended by Love?

How did Martha balance the tension of what she expected her sister to do and what her sister actually did? Did her observation of

Mary's actions become judgment statements, assaults on her character, blame? Was Martha seeking to shame her sister, use Mary's perceived flaws to force what she wanted? How did Martha hold the tension when Jesus did not respond to her request to use his authority to make a paternalistic demand of Mary?

There was so much not said about Mary in what Martha did say.

And there's so much left to infer in between the lines. For example, we don't know if Martha grumbled under her breath. I know I would have if I were the one slaving away unaided in the kitchen, weighed down by perfectionism, performative behavior, and societal norms.

But this is the thing about the text: Sometimes it says a lot about our complexity as humans without saying much at all, even between the lines of what's not said.

For example, when relationships are ruled by a sense of hierarchy and dominance of power, it breeds disconnection and distance. When hierarchy is abolished, relational dynamics shift and each participant is 100 percent responsible for their part in maintaining connection, meaning they get to choose. I'm no longer doing this because I *should*, or because someone told me it's the *right* thing to do, or what I am supposed to do.

Obligation is off the table when Love abounds because Love always recognizes the gift of choice and honors one's freedom to choose.

Martha demanded that Jesus correct Mary. "You have the power, Jesus. Force her to do what I want her to do."

But that's judgments and expectations, right?

We get all up in our heads about how a person should be, should act, what they should do—and shoulding all over everything, we birth expectations from these convictions of our own expert opinion.

These are projections, really, of my own imagination. The story I've told myself is based on my culture, my background, my religious upbringing, the standards and norms I hold myself to—all these things factor into how we react or respond in certain situations and then consciously (more often, unconsciously) demand that same response from others. "Do it my way or suffer my disappointment."

How did Martha manage herself in this exchange? Did she huff and slam serving trays so Jesus and the others, especially Mary, *heard* her disenchantment? How else would the writer know she was frantic in the kitchen? Did she get mad at Jesus's response, or did it trigger a moment of remembrance? Did she come to herself, take a deep breath, and own the part she had chosen?

Again, we don't necessarily know. We only know that Martha was feeling some kind of way that she was in the kitchen and her sister was not. When she asked Jesus to reprimand Mary and essentially take her side, he did not. Instead, Jesus tells Martha that Mary had chosen the best part.

Is that to say serving is bad? Making sure your guest has food not a desirable choice? Absolutely not.

So what did Martha do with Jesus's response? Did it fuel more judgment statements, shoulds, and injured expectations? Did she own the way she felt and surrender to the moment, yield to acceptance?

As I stated earlier, many preachers have gone down a rabbit hole of filling in the blanks on what Jesus's response meant and what we should take away from these few verses. I don't want to join them, but I'm struck by the opportunity in this story for us to wrestle with what we do when things don't go our way, when we have expectations of people to act with decency, honor their responsibility, do what they *should* do—but they don't.

Sometimes it's easier to act out—get frantic, get mad, cuss people out, cut people off—than to own and name what we feel. Like manipulation and control, displays of anger and brashness are often tools we pick up to avoid the hard work of dealing with ourselves.

We avoid asking ourselves, "Why? Why do I need you to do what I want you to do? Why do I need you to believe what I believe the way I believe it or use the same language I use?"

Why is sameness so comforting that we set out to recreate the world in our image, with our likes and preferences? Why do we buy into the lie that we can control people? Why have we tied our sense of safety to getting the outcome we most desire instead of trusting in Love's goodness?

I wonder: How might this story have been rewritten if Martha had been able to give herself the validation and permission she wanted Jesus to issue?

What if she was able to acknowledge her feelings—the power and depth of each one, to give them space to roll through her, to breathe and take on life, to be able to articulate well what was going on inside: "Jesus, I feel left out. I feel alone, abandoned. I feel trapped in gender roles that require me to serve when I too want to sit at your feet and glean," or "Mary, when you leave me to handle all the preparation of the meal by myself, I feel angry. I feel frustrated under the burden of having to get it right, get the food out in a timely manner."

How might our stories be rewritten if we were more versed in heart language? What if we lived unafraid, unashamed to hand someone a sacred part of our internal world? Completely aware that vulnerability can sometimes feel like running naked through a packed gymnasium, still we decide to trust someone else inside the place where we process our pain and how things are affecting us.

What if we felt our feelings instead of disconnecting from them? We use a lot of body analogies but live very disembodied realities.

Connection happens when you hear my heart: when you hold my heart with deep regard, and I respond in like manner to you. We share how we feel to create opportunities for being known.

One of the most valuable gifts a person can give to someone who says, "I feel..." is compassionate listening.

Feelings don't require fixing.

You may feel discomfort in not fixing, in the raw expression of another's feelings. That is okay.

Discomfort is a necessary tension that helps facilitate growth opportunities. When discomfort arises, touch your heart or the place on your body where you are noticing discomfort. Take a deep, cleansing breath and offer yourself reassurance: "This is a moment of discomfort. Such moments are common in the world. Even in my discomfort, lovingkindness sustains me. And I offer lovingkindness to others impacted by this moment as well."

As a Black person and one who aspires to follow the Way of Love, in my wrestle with injustice, sometimes I struggle to remember that even those who jump on the bandwagon of what I think are silly theories, those who deny systemic racism exists, or those who choose to be silent in the face of ongoing oppression and police brutality are God's beloved too.

I am Martha, frantic in my rightness, wanting my brothers and sisters of lighter melanin to jump in the kitchen and help me. Let's work this out together. I don't want to serve alone. I don't want to clean up this mess alone. I want to sit and glean too, but there is so much work to be done.

I am Martha wanting something of Jesus. "Jesus, speak to my sister. Speak to my brother. Tell them to help me. I shouldn't be the only one preparing the food, serving the meal. You're the authority here; command them to get to work."

I am Martha, with a history of slights—whether race related or gender related—overlooked, forgotten, and relegated to the kitchen. Invisible threads that weave the fabric of my lived experiences are begging to be seen, to be acknowledged by someone outside of myself. Do I stew in overwhelm until I blow my top, storm out of the kitchen, and interrupt whatever is being said—make my hurts known, demand to be heard because I've suffered under the weight of my own plot hole, and what's happening inside of me can no longer wait? I need the outcome I imagined, and I need it right now. "Jesus, can't you, of all people, see? Tell my sister to help me."

I am Martha. We have suffered in silence, unseen for far too long.

I am Martha—grumbling, slamming things, often with a lot of expletives, to make sure everyone knows I am upset with Mary—and, if I'm honest, with Jesus too. After all, didn't I expect him to take my side?

How do I move from upset to right alignment, from frustration to restoration? How do I marvel with awe at the transcendent, staring into the bowels of hell? How do I resolve the tension?

How do I move to the place where I'm remembering this person is a burning bush, a sign and a wonder, not an irritant?

For me, judgments, assumptions, and expectations cloud the lens of my heart, and when I'm staring out at the world through a dirty lens, there's no amount of changing what I see until I clean the lens. When my eye is not clear and my body is not full of light, I realize my need to gaze into the eyes of Love.

Only Love burns away the whispers, the judgments, the expectations, the demands, the desire for what I perceive to be right. Only Love tends the wound of offense.

Even in the story of Mary and Martha, when I gaze into the eyes of Love, I find hidden underneath the surface of Martha's frustration, the weightiness of her burden, that another truth is incubating, waiting to yield its fruit.

In Jesus's response, I don't hear a denial or even a dismissal of Martha's angst. I hear an invitation: *"Only one thing matters. Mary has chosen the best part, and it's not going to be taken away from her."*[24]

You can also choose the best part, Martha, and neither will it be taken away from you.

Could it be that choosing the good part unburdens us of our dogged determination to control the outcome of other people's actions?

---

24. Luke 10:42 (NTE).

Instead, I am Martha, projecting outward, looking for resolution, missing the invitation to sit with Spirit in my feelings, breathe through them—allow them to be as they are within me without judgment or shame. To be present in my body, with my body.

Like Martha, could Jesus be inviting us to consider a different way? There she is, likely feeling angst and animosity, a desire to lash out at her sister, perhaps respond ruthlessly. But rather than scold Mary herself, Martha beseeches Jesus to command Mary, and instead of giving back to Martha what she expects to receive, he offers her a choice.

And I know I keep coming back to that point, but I'm struck by how much has stayed the same in relational dynamics from the writing of that story until now. We still look for someone we perceive has power to save us, to fix our life.

External validation. External permission. External controls.

Martha, what will you choose? How will you orient yourself? Will the way you interact in this relationship lead to further demise or to healing? Will you choose the Way of Love?

Gazing into the eyes of Love does not deny that sometimes we need a little help in the kitchen. The Way of Love does not deny our pain or the need for continued reform in policies and systems. Nor does the Way of Love mitigate the complexities of the issues our communities continue to face. But it does free us from the narrative of the negative, from demanding that others conform to performative behavior that best aligns with our ideals.

"Mary has chosen the best part, and it's not going to be taken away from her."

Martha, will you pause your doing, fulfilling your societal roles, your shoulds, and your narratives long enough to gaze into the eyes of Love?

Will you allow Love to inform the way you relate to others, the way you live and move and have your being in the world?

What do we glean from Love when we still our busyness enough to rest, to be still and know?

What will rise as we gaze into the eyes of Love?

Tender mercy, perhaps. Compassion. Unconditional acceptance. Lovingkindness. Understanding.

May our judgments, assumptions, and expectations bow their knee as we sit at the feet of Jesus and gaze into the eyes of Love. May it be so, Lord. May it be so.

If you're silent,

You can hear the forest breathe,

The holy hush of the trees' limbs.

"Silence," wrote Thomas Keating, "is God's first language"[25]:

the way it soaks into your skin,

surrounds you,

blanketing you like the forest's breath.

Silence:

the cadence of the land at rest,

the body asleep,

the heart awake.

Silence:

the deep rhythmic breathing of a mind slowed down,

an ocean still,

wet dew clinging to grass blade.

Silence:

the sacred song trapped in a bird's breast before its first chirp,

the still of night across a desert landscape,

wrapped in a bone-aching chill

before the sun rises to scorch its parched earth.

Silence:

---

25. Thomas Keating, *Intimacy with God* (New York: Crossroad, 1994), 55.

the lusty gaze of onlookers staring at the negro on the lynching tree,

neck snapped,

life ended,

feet dangling, back and forth,

back and forth.

Silenced:

Hands up, don't shoot!

Body thrumming with a heady sense of power.

Hands in pocket,

resting pose, knees embedded into a man's neck.

Silence, please.

I. Can't. Breathe,

Silenced.[26]

We are trying to achieve with our head something that can only ever be accomplished in our hearts.

Our heart is who we are; it is the place of memory,

the place of remembering,

the place where our inner truth abides.

---

26. A version of this poem was published as "Silence" in *Oneing* 9, no. 1 (Spring 2021), 19–20.

Still yourself enough to allow Truth to rise from your innermost being.

Then tell your story.

Listen to someone else's story.

As you listen, hold with tenderness the differences.

Revel with awe at our shared commonalities and points of intersection.

Build relationships, genuine relationships of mutuality with one another.

We cannot shame or shock or guilt our way into a reconciled reality.

It won't work.

Stats and facts don't heal. Love does.

Anger and hate

pull us into separateness,

divide us from one another.

The earth is groaning

for us to open our hearts,

and unveil the truth.

We all are closely connected.

Therein lies peace.

Even in the face of strong disagreement on ideals and policies,

may we pause and remember

that we are interconnected.

Humanity, sentient beings,

creation, cosmos, and Creator

—the thread of Love weaves through us all.

In the face of great love

and/or

great suffering,

may we lean into the best of who we are

with humility and grace.

May kindness and compassion arise.

A CALL TO ACTION

Open your eyes and see humanity.

Target your community and infiltrate it with love and hope.

Seek to understand.

Attend your local civic league. Know the people who are making decisions in your neighborhood and district.

+ Buy a LEO (law enforcement officer) lunch and have a conversation. Ask disarming questions.

+ Gather three couples from other ethnic groups and/or religions and host a dinner for eight. Learn about one another's culture, histories, struggles, and successes. Make it a potluck featuring cultural dishes and use the story of food and family to guide your knowing.

+ For those of you who feel called to simply pray, great. Go prayer-walk in an indigent neighborhood with gloved hands and a trash bag and pick up trash as you pray.

+ Spend an hour in a Title I school as a tutor or teacher's helper.

+ No time in your workday to be hands-on? Take a twenty-dollar bill and offer it to a teacher in said school to help her buy classroom supplies. Or give it to the cafeteria manager and ask her to put it on the books of a child who is struggling to pay for lunch.

- Read *Just Mercy*[27] by Bryan Stevenson to educate yourself. Learn more about restorative justice practices and how you can get involved.

- Realize that your acknowledgment of someone's pain, without justification or defense of what caused the pain, is like air to a suffocating person. Look in the face of someone who doesn't look like you and say, "I see you. I hear you. I don't know your pain firsthand, but I'm sorry you've had that experience."

Still not sure how you can help or what you can do?

Get quiet. Ask Spirit: Spirit, how can I help someone lay down tonight and sleep without fear? Spirit, what does love, expressed through my life, look like? Spirit, how do I stand in solidarity with the hurting?

"Love, what does your *body broken* look like in our community today?" And then listen...because Love looks like something.

---

27. Bryan Stevenson, *Just Mercy: A Story of Justice and Redemption* (New York: One World/Random House, 2015).

Sometimes I'm judgy. I've been hurt by people—hurt people; insecure people; wounded people; people hungry for power, position, and sometimes profit; and yes, even good people. Nevertheless, that harm has left me slightly suspicious. So I judge.

Beyond a mechanism to self-protect, how does my judging serve me?

If I close my eyes and scan my body, I find it taut, ready to spring. Tension and tightness are lacing my shoulders, neck. Lips pursed. Jaw clenched. Elbows locked. Fingers balled into fists. Breath short. Eyes laser focused, assessing, calculating. This is my defensive battle stance, my posture of resistance.

I inhale and listen to what my body wants to tell me:

Gurl, I am tired. I am exhausted. Who has hurt us so deeply that we always have to live coiled, ready to attack? Remind me again, who are we afraid of? What are we afraid of? I am soul weary, tired of being leery. Surely there is another way for us to live, 'cause this judging thing—calculating, assessing, always counting and measuring—this is going to lead to our demise.

The intensity of our battle stance is manifesting in me: inflammation, skin irritation, insomnia, indigestion. We are fighting against ourselves in ways that are not healthy.

What if, instead of imagining the worst and creating stories of possible torment that keep us in a heightened state of resistance, we start to tell ourselves a different narrative? What if we yield to the mystery of Love? What would acceptance feel like in our body? Trust? Surrender? What if our eyes became portals of nonjudgmental awareness? What if we used our brain for something other than forming opinions that deepen suspicion and mistrust? I wanna live. I wanna love.

And this, this "always being wary of the other" stance, this is not living. We are breaking down.

I touch my body gently: my jiggly thighs, my round belly, soft breasts. Lingering over the area of my heart, I breathe in, receiving this insight from my body. What would it be like to lay aside judgment after a history of injured expectations and wounded assumptions? I'm uncertain. But I realize I can't freely go forward until I understand where I've been.

So I take a physical step back, a symbolic somatic gesture into my past.

Closing my eyes once more, I turn to my body. "Body, there are experiences, responses to words and actions of others that you've held in order for me to live, and I trust you know when we're ready to deal with what we've repressed. Is now the time for you to share some of those things with me?"

I want to ask, "When did this all begin, why did this all begin?" Instead, I surrender and ask: "Body, what do you want me to know?"

How many times were we blamed for things we didn't do? How many times have we been wronged or felt misunderstood? How long have we carried the burden of false responsibility? If "all your fault" was a poster child, we would be America's next top model. And so, we learned to read people and situations, to calculate, observe, assess. But what happens when we turn our observations into narratives, our assessments into judgments? When the mind spins, creating stories we tell ourselves, we tend to wrest control of the narrative, turning people into fictive characters, forcing them into outcomes we've already imagined. Blanks filled in, certainties assured, this leaves no room for the mystery of Love. No room for compassion…or growth. No room for change or the possibility that we might be wrong about the opinions we've formed. Could we possibly be creating people in the image of our judgments and not as they truly are? Are we doing the very thing we didn't want done to us?

"'The mystery of Love'? What are you really saying, body? Are you saying we're turning people into villains to resist them, to justify our defensive posture?"

I am your body. We are one. My job is to support us, to be the hug that keeps us upright, to store in our cells the memory of our days, and...to turn our hearts back to the mystery of Love: to ideas and ancient practices that support our wholeness, to ways of being that lead to freedom and invite us to live in the fullness of our humanity. There is a way out of exhaustion, suspicion, and judgment.

"And what way is that, body?"

Let our story begin and end with Love. Let Love be the pause, the period, the high-water mark, and the exclamation points that dot the narratives we tell ourselves. Offer the benefit of the doubt. Allow the mystery of Love to fill in the blanks instead of suspicion and judgment. Let us listen to the unsaid with our heart and not our suspicions. How do we find our way out of exhaustion and judgment? Grace.

I don't like being around people who once made me feel like sh*t.

Even if I was the one creating the narrative about what I thought they thought about me, it doesn't make being around these people any easier.

Sh*t stink lingers on the fingers long after you've washed your hands.

And sometimes it's hard to separate actual people from the story you've told yourself about those people.

But this is the arduous, *brutiful* (brutal plus beautiful) work of healing: the separating, the unraveling. Unbinding yourself from narratives that perpetuate bitterness.

As we surrender to Love's perfect work, the fury of Love is aimed at everything that is not of Love's kind.

We're stripping away all the muck that dims our unique expression as image bearers, including the narratives we tell ourselves to protect ourselves from other people's character defects.

The things in my life, in your life, that happened, happened. Nothing diminishes the veracity of your experience.

The change Love invites us into is how we live and move and have our being in spite of—or rather, because of—the things that have happened to us.

How do I exist in my body in a way that isn't fragmented or stunted?

For me, when sh*t stink lingers on my fingers, my defended self goes into warrior mode—distancing, walling off, hiding out, doing whatever feels right to protect herself from pain, from hurt and harm.

Whenever I catch a whiff of that foul smell, I know it's an invitation to pause, to touch my heart, to name fear, to feel my feet supported by the earth, to express gratitude for the self who survived hell and has lived to tell it.

This does not always silence the stories, but like the eye of the storm, in the center, all is calm. And from this grounded state, I tell my mind: I will not live trapped in a story of my own making, and I offer myself compassion.

As Tara Brach writes, "Compassion honors our experience; it allows us to be intimate with the life of this moment as it is. Compassion makes our acceptance wholehearted and complete."[28]

Politics and othering paradigms are energy leeches, and it's so easy to get sucked into the madness of the matrix.

Ask Spirit to show you where you've willfully participated through negative thoughts and actions. Call back your energy from those negative missions.

Everything in and about our lives runs off the fuel of our hearts. Be still and quiet your heart. After a few deep breaths, ask yourself:

+ Where am I thinking like a wounded child?

---

28. Tara Brach, *Radical Acceptance: Embracing Your Life with the Heart of a Buddha* (New York: Bantam: 2003), 28, 200–201.

- Where do I still have attachments to past negative experiences and negative beliefs?

- How are my judgments of other people being synthesized in my body?

Call back your spirit from the past and release the negative influence of all your wounds. While this heart work may take a while to filter into your body or result in healing, just pausing to be still and doing the work that leads to wholeness is a peaceful thing on its own.

Judgment statements are thinking statements. They are statements of opinion birthed from what we think someone should do or say, or how we think someone should act or interpret data and facts.

Judgments and *shoulds* are largely formed from injured expectations. This means we project onto others how we would react or respond in a certain situation and consciously (or, more often, unconsciously) demand that behavior from others.

This is why we instinctively pursue agreement over connection. It's the place of homogeneous thinking, feeling, and behaving. Agreement creates a cocoon of false safety.

Unconditional acceptance says, "I'm not them, they aren't me." It frees others from my expectation that they handle life the way I would.

People often refrain from sharing because they fear being judged. Perfect love displaces fear.

Feeling statements are the language of the heart.

While no one else is responsible for how I feel, when I hand someone my feelings in conversation, I'm handing them a sacred part of my internal world. It's the place of how the things I'm processing are affecting me.

Connection happens when a person hears my heart and can hold the tender concerns of my heart with deep regard. Reciprocity happens when I respond in like manner.

Feelings don't require fixing. We share how we feel to create opportunities to be known.

The most valuable gift a person can give to someone who says, "I feel…" is compassionate listening.

Squeeze their hand. Hug their neck.

Share their pain with your own tears.

Look them in the eye, silently, and listen.

I see you. I hear you. I'm with you.

The gift of yoga (holy union):

Your body will speak to you.

If you silence the self-criticism and judgment long enough, it will finally say what the voices of others and the voices in your own head have kept it from saying.

Your body will tell you it is amazing.

Your body will tell you it is strong.

When you are in tune with your body, your body can do all kinds of amazing and strong things.

Your body will tell you not to compare itself to others,

that bodies come in all shapes and sizes.

Who told you your body was something to hide, shame, and cover up because it's bigger or smaller in size than another—

Who told you that?

Who told you

your thighs were too big,

your butt too wide,

your breasts

too saggy, too full, too small, too little—

Who told you that?

Where did you learn to hide,

to be ashamed,

and when will you ever stop?

Why not now?

Why not stop today,

this moment?

Body, you are a gift to me

and I'm through judging you.

I will spend my days unwrapping and exploring,

embracing and appreciating who you are,

and when the voices creep in,

telling me you're too this, too that,

not enough of this,

that you should hide that

or cover up this—

I will pause,

I will breathe,

and I will ask:

Body, what say you?

And I will no longer war against you

with the opinions of others.

I will align my soul and my spirit

to be in holy union with you.

One day I decided it was better to integrate all of me, to applaud my best effort—even in my messy brokenness—than to keep trying to cut away the past parts that I didn't like so much.

After all, fragmentation contributes to dissociative identity disorder, and I'm exhausted being a chameleon.

My past self served me, protected me, hid me, and worked hand in hand with Divine Love to guide me to who I am today.

One of the best days of my life was the day I looked in the mirror and said, "I'm no longer resisting you. I'm no longer fighting against the journey of where you're taking me. Thank you for leading us to this place. You were everything I needed in the moment I needed it. Forgive me for hating you, for fighting against you, for trying to turn you into someone and something that you're not."

My past self smiled back at me and said, "For a time, you walked outside your name, unaware of who you truly are. There will be more times of that, though not as many, for now you're alive to the thrum of Love, and you know how to still yourself where you once did not. It's been an honor to be you. We got this."

Our wink was simultaneous because my past self and I are one.

My heart quivers.

My stomach flutters.

My head knows, but the other body centers don't often line up as quickly as I would like.

I feel the resistance:

My feet rooting into the ground,

set to fight

set to flight

looking longingly in the distance

for whatever could ease the ache.

Somewhere in my brain, a memory roots:

It won't always be this way.

It won't always feel this heavy.

You won't always want to flee.

You won't always feel alone.

I sit on my mat,

becoming familiar with the resistance coursing through my body.

Deep inhale.

Deep exhale.

I sit.

I acknowledge.

I lament.

I accept.

With deep breaths, I return my eyes

to what has been set before me.

It is what it is....

It is as it is....

It is as it should be....

I open my hands and my heart to this present moment.

With acceptance, I say yes.

I forward fold, bowing my steely head beneath my heart and gut.

Deep inhale.

It is what it is....

I stand like a tree,

poised in my body—head, heart, and gut aligned.

It is as it is....

I bend back, palms splayed, and greet my present reality.

Deep breath: We got this.

It is as it should be.

Why cast down, Dear Soul?

And why are you disquieted within me?

Why is your breath short, your lungs constricted?

Dear Soul, I feel the pain of your anguish in the sensations of my body. I feel your restlessness—the desire for the dark night to end and day to break forth.

Dear Soul, I feel your yearning, your angst, and how normalcy feels like the place we should return to. But this is the thing about journeying, Dear Soul. The dark night of liminality is more womb than tomb: a birthing canal and invitation to cross the threshold of what was into the light of a new day, a new beginning.

This is not a reconstructed reset of a regurgitated past experience.

No, Dear Soul, the womb of the dark night is a space where life is held, where seeds are nourished, kept safe in their gestation. Without connection, wombs could not exist.

And I know, Dear Soul, this time has seemed like one of bleak, utter loneliness—the antithesis of connection. But in the womb, life flows from the Host, connected and held together by a cord. Life passing to life, and sometimes that is all that binds us to one another and to life itself. And it too, this thread of the Master Weaver, this thread of love is enough.

Scarcity would have us believe differently. Scarcity demands certainty for survival. Scarcity robs us of a confidence to trust our Host in the dark night.

The dark may linger a while longer. We are promised both rain and sunshine. But this I know, Dear Soul: No element shall ever sever the cord that binds you to our Host, Divine Love—not alienation, not disquiet, not even unrest.

This is the thing, Dear Soul. We are unaware of so much that happens in the dark. The dark greets us with an invitation to embrace mystery. The dark is the place where Love asks us to trust, to yield and surrender.

Take a pause, Dear Soul, a long inhale of breath and release. Where does that land in your body? What do you feel of Love's invitation to surrender and trust? How has this dark night been womb-like for you? What is growing and expanding within you?

You see, Dear Soul, underneath the unrest and chatter, Love is doing what Love always does: steadying you, holding you, supporting you. Even when you feel off the rails and flailing about, Love is there.

Dear Soul, Love is our anchor, our sounding board for truth-telling. Love is our plumb line, the bulwark, our calm in a turbulent sea.

As we close our eyes and envision home amid the dark, may our souls feel Love's calming presence. With each long inhale and reciprocal exhale, touching with deep tenderness any agitated sensations that are rising in the body, may our souls feel the comfort of Love.

May you settle, Dear Soul, into Love's embrace.

May you quiet as you rest in Love's generosity.

You are here, and you are held.

The body is a holy enigma.

One to embrace with eyes and heart wide open.

I will not dishonor, shame, or judge

the beautiful rolls that sustain me, hold me,

trap my emotions when I'm not yet ready to process.

Hips wide to support my girth,

belly soft

face full.

This is me.

I am here.

I am alive.

In the 1978 movie *The Wiz*,[29] the iconic Diana Ross sings, "When I think of home, I think of a place where there's love overflowing."[30]

What rises in your body when you think of home? Is home synonymous with love and affection? Is home a place you long to return to?

For some, home is terror, a place to flee with no desire to return or revisit. This is important to name and acknowledge because too many are aimlessly wandering, feeling insignificant—unseen, unknown.

When home is not a place of comfort, and there is no sense of knowing or nurture, it leaves the body in flight-or-fight mode. We see this in Dorothy's companions, the scarecrow and the cowardly lion. One runs to isolation, invisibility, and separation, choosing to hide. The other blusters to cover a lack of courage, choosing to demand a place in the world with a body that remains on full alert, suspicious and defensive. Whether self-protecting or hiding, one thing is true: Neither posture offers the soul any type of rest. Neither is home.

Often, when we think of *home*, we think only of an external place, out there, a fixed place—the place where we live and grow, create fond memories, establish familial bonds; the place we leave when we come of age and where we return when things are hard.

The evolution of Dorothy's journey on the yellow brick road expands home beyond the narrow confines of a fixed place to a vast inward sea. "I've learned," she says, "that we must look inside our hearts to find a world full of love...like home."[31]

29. *The Wiz*, directed by Sidney Lumet (1978; Universal Pictures).
30. L. Frank Baum, William F. Brown, and Joel Schumacher, *The Wiz* (Detroit: Motown Productions, 1978), www.imdb.com/title/tt0078504/quotes/?ref_=tt_trv_qu.
31. Ibid.

Love is home.

Home is both an external dwelling and an internal abode. Home is the place where we belong, our place of acceptance and welcome. There, in this shame and judgment-free embryonic cocoon of love, we practice unconditional acceptance; we learn to relate to ourselves and the world around us.

And home is a soft place for the body to land, a safe place for the soul to fully disrobe. Home is the place where our failures don't kill, our sins can't crush, and even when we are at our worst, we're safe. Home is a place where we are free to take our deepest, fullest, least encumbered breath.

At home, there's no need to guess whether we're in or out, welcomed or not. Home always prepares a place with us in mind.

How are you preparing a home of unconditional acceptance for yourself? How do you welcome your body, make room for your mind? In what ways are you engaging your soul with intentionality? How are you reclaiming the safety of home for yourself?

"Home," says Glinda the Good, "is a place we all must find. It's not just a place where you eat or sleep. Home is knowing: knowing your mind, knowing your heart, knowing your courage. If we know ourselves, we're always home, anywhere."[32]

How do we curate home?

When the wizard seeks Dorothy's counsel, she tells him, "I don't know what's in you. You'll have to find that out for yourself. And you'll have to begin by letting people see who you really are."[33]

How do we come home to ourselves? Knowing our mind. Knowing our heart. Owning our courage. And then, we allow others to see who we really are.

---

32. Ibid.
33. Ibid.

If hurting is based on seeing all that is not myself

as other

then, I fully want to see.

Into the waters I go,

to be reborn,

baptized in infinite grace,

Immersed in infinite Love,

swept up in the tide of infinite mercy.

The infinite limitlessness of the Ground of All Being,

an unending shore,

constantly inviting me

to awaken to the infinite.

I am that which has always existed within me:

no division

no separation

holy whole—each chasm bridged,

every fragment forged into home.

I see what always was.

There is nothing outside myself

that is not me.

We are woven together for eternity.

Being human is the gift.

The day we give ourselves permission to *be*, without being afraid of ourselves or afraid that we're inauthentic because we're messy, is the day we find utter freedom.

Give yourself permission to unfold—to doubt, to fear, to marvel, to question, to be sad, to be angry, to live in wonder, to be joyful, to change your mind, to be content...to experience the breadth and depth of your full humanity.

Too often, we see our bodies as something to be used, consumed, and beaten into submission.

We spend our lives pining away for some thing, some talent, some creative expression to be deemed as our *gift*, our purpose...the *it* for which we were born. "If I could just discover *it*, I'll be okay. I'll find my worth. I'll feel significant—*useful*."

When you realize that *you* are the gift, every expression of your being *is* purposeful. *Be*-ing is participating with Divine Love, and that alone is *the* gift, first to yourself and then to others and all of creation.

Transaction aside, when I surrender to being me and understanding the gift that I am, I settle more deeply into my skin and bones and sink into a cosmic okay-ness. This is the redemptive beauty of incarnate living—to fully embody myself as I join with Love.

Shame is like an autoimmune disease. It turns us against ourselves.

The first instinct of a body riddled with shame is to conceal and hide.

But we were made for freedom.

To be free, we must release ourselves from the grip of patriarchal domination.

To be free, it is essential to become aware of how we are disconnected from our bodies.

Who taught us to hate our bodies, to judge the way we look, the way we're shaped?

How do they benefit from our disconnection?

Pause and think about it:

+ How has your body cared for you?
+ How has it held you?
+ In what ways has your body supported you?
+ How have you repaid it—with judgment, criticism, curses, or with something far more beautiful?

Our bodies are not our enemies.

May we offer our bodies the same tenderness and compassion we offer to others.

And may we offer to the earth a similar kindness as well.

Since I was seventeen, I have lived my life trying to escape a part of my reality.

One past conversation led me to text my husband: **I hate this part of my life. I hate it. Please let me move to Siberia.**

On and on I ranted.

To which my husband Doug kindly replied: **I'm in a meeting, but let's revisit this.**

(Gotta love being married to a pastoral person.)

In the absence of my human sounding board, I turned to mindfulness. I asked my heart, "Why? Why do you keep trying to run? What about that part of your life is so bad that it prevents you from being?"

I took several deep, cleansing breaths, allowing myself to feel the angst and weight of every emotion and all the inner turmoil my heart was experiencing.

As each breath deepened, I felt my heart settle. My chest became less tight, and the emotions of negation began to pass through me as the energy changed within.

Truthfully, I don't know that I'll ever lose the desire to run, to be free of perceived constraints and expectations. But I am learning I can choose how I respond when the little girl inside is triggered.

May I be free.   May you be free.

May I be at peace.   May you be at peace.

May my heart settle into Love's rhythm.

May your heart settle into Love's rhythm.

You can fight,

you can flee, or

you can heal.

When the vortex of chaos tries to suck you into its whirlwind, close your eyes and inhale deeply.

Notice where tension is rising in your body.

Drop your shoulders, slow exhale.

Remember, this is a moment, not an eternity.

May your soul say, "Yes, I remember.

In Love, I live and move and have my being."

Am I loving?

Am I including all?

Am I abounding in grace?

Am I walking in freedom and allowing others the opportunity to be free?

Am I letting go of that which no longer serves me?

Am I clinging to certitude or remaining open to transformation?

What you choose in your heart and what you say *yes* to may not always feel like an external win as it relates to other people and relational dynamics.

You may find yourself asking, "Am I being selfish, unconcerned, disconnected? Could I handle this better?"

Realize that when you're dealing with dysfunction and brokenness, your *good* will often get twisted and misconstrued.

It takes Divine Love to keep us grounded in Truth instead of conforming to the demands that fear of man will attempt to yoke upon us.

That place of Divine Love breeds confidence to be more for wholeness than for participating in someone else's drama.

A firm, "No, I will not co-sign on your dark, twisted, broken version of love," is a choice to cut the cords that bind us to codependency and life as an enabler.

When we no longer need a hero's high and give ourselves permission to redefine who we are, devoid of a savior complex, the conflict and tension behind our *yes* and the decisions we make for our personal sanity and peace of mind will slowly dissipate.

Deserving—counting and measuring,

success, failure—counting and measuring:

finite ways of valuing our ego.

Consciously, we'd never desire our win to come at the expense of someone else's loss.

But isn't that the game of competition?

Counting and measuring:

win some, lose some.

We miss the mark,

but fail to question:

Who set it?

Who boxes us in to finite existence?

The measure of our personhood weighed in wins,

cars, Gucci, houses, pearls.

Likes, followers, influencer status

holds nothing on the sacredness of our holy self.

Ways of counting and measuring

weighing on the soul, settling into the body:

fear

lack

Standing opposite one another:

outside

over Against

divided by the space between,

outside of myself,

I'm sizing up the other,

counting and measuring,

weighing our differences,

determining which is preferred,

which is better.

Will the ego feel superior,

or

like a failure?

I remember watching my dad as he lay dying in hospice. Attempting to wrangle the most out of each precious moment, I watched his blanket with fierce intensity, savoring each rise and fall of the coverlet. Each held breath was filled with precious memories and unspoken words, both mine and his. Longing was trapped between us: longing for more time, for a different outcome, for do-overs. I could have easily fallen into a rabbit hole with my grief, consumed by what was on the horizon. Thankfully, I'd had enough mindfulness training that what arrested me most was the desire to savor each moment with Dad as if that one moment might be our last together.

I studied him as he slept. I noticed more deeply his hands and toes when I assisted him. I listened more intently for his breathing amid the moans. And while he was still lucid, I paid careful attention to his requests, his words. Slowing down to savor and being mindfully present eased the ache of longing.

What do you long for? What lingers on your tongue? Whose scent remains long after a deep hug or coupling? Which memories of pleasure have burrowed their way into your psyche like grit underneath your fingernails?

Close your eyes. Inhale deeply. What do your senses conjure?

Perhaps long walks in the park.

Hands held.

A nearness so close, your hip bones touch.

The intensity of a mother's eyes locked on the face of her newborn.

The smell of Sunday dinner: pot roast and cabbage.

An uncorked bottle of wine,

left open to breathe.

Summer rain.

Freshly mowed grass.

Earth turned over, ready for seed and mulch.

To savor is to participate in the wonder of noticing:

to see

to appreciate

to love.

In a world that walks swiftly, unconsciously, largely moving by rote muscle memory and habitual patterns through the cares and normalcy of life, I wonder: What invites us to pause? What wonderful, majestic moment creates a disruption big enough to savor? And how could moments become mindful intention so that we are present in our lives in ways that make savoring a constancy?

We rush to devour, to sate our lust.

Unhurried, we linger to savor,

exploring the unexplored with controlled discipline,

taking it all in, filling our senses,

relishing in the taste, touch, feel, smell, and sight of someone

or some thing's presence

being thoroughly and utterly enjoyed.

Relishing instead of ravishing.

Savoring instead of devouring.

Yet, I wonder: How might the Divine be inviting us to savor the beauty of the world around us, to delight with utter enjoyment in the diversity of bodies around us, and how would our world differ if we savored one another's unique personhood with the same fascination and appreciation for beauty and awe that we offer when savoring nature, or a meal, or a moment?

What is it to look in the face of another and savor what we see, to be moved to linger with such controlled discipline that we couldn't turn away if we tried, arrested by the majesty of our beholding?

What can savoring teach us that fast consumption and hurried unconscious movement don't?

What if we held tenderly the rise and fall of each breath flowing in the breast of another? How might it ease the longing trapped between us?

*Many people think that they understand others when they
merely maintain a kindly attitude toward them. While it is
true that a generous mood toward other people again and again
elicits a response of friendliness, this is no substitute for facts,
for information and the kind of understanding which comes
only from sustained natural exposure to others. This constant
exposure is apt to be a sure check and corrective to one's under-
standing…We can be so earnest and sincere in our grim deter-
mination to be brotherly that we are completely unmindful of
the effect of our action on those whom it is our greatest desire to
understand…Human understanding requires great artistry…
This is one of the reasons why conversation and good talk are of
such immense value.*[34]
—Howard Thurman

Can I make space for another to share their truth and hold the
weight of their pain without judging, without fear or concern for how
their truth-telling makes me look (or feel), or without shifting under
the discomfort of their passionate emotions?

Less in our head,

more in our body.

Less in our perceptions,

more in our lived experience.

34. Howard Thurman, *Deep Is the Hunger: Meditations for Apostles of Sensitiveness*
(New York: Harper & Row, 1951; Richmond, IN: Friends United Press, 1978),
23–24.

Less in our narratives,

    more in our facts.

Less in our othering,

    more in our conversing.

Moving to judgment too quickly restricts curiosity.

How and why is where the healing happens.

Make peace with not understanding.

Make peace with difference.

Make peace with your body.

There are good secrets, and there are bad.

Secrets rise to the fore, unbidden. I hear the exhale of my breath, its sharp intake. I feel my heart lodged against the back of my throat. What are these secrets asking of me? Who are they asking me to be?

Feel, the secrets beg. *Remember*, the secrets invoke. Tears prick my eyes.

My body is full of secrets. Some, I can explain. Some, I cannot.

Some, I've let hit the air. The need for them to diminish, to release their power over me, is great. Some, I have stitched to my ribs, hidden inside, in the depth of my being, where words and understanding would fail to illuminate the magnitude of their significance.

There are secrets…and then there are secrets. We all have secrets.

Some secrets are dark, cutting into the body like stinging, freshly etched tattoos. Blade after blade, dug deep, they pierce through to the soul.

Damn the secrets shut up in my bone. How do I yield to their beseeching?

Every buried secret deepens the chasm between communal intimacy and me. How can I allow myself to be witnessed when the secrets blind my own self-sight? How do I offer myself the courage to be present with these secrets—the ones that scare me and the ones I scare by turning my attention toward them? I must first witness myself apart from the stitching of these secrets: unweave, unbind.

May the kiss of Love sustain me in my brokenness, that I might cross the chasm between my secrets and me. Come close enough to touch the thread that binds them tightly, knit so fastidiously that some feel as if they've always been with me.

If I can't touch them, I can't heal them.

When the shadows fade and the lights dim and there's no one but me, am I in my skin or in my secrets? My feet tingle. My legs thrum. My lips prick. There is a cord of tightness along my neck. My body is clothed in skin and secrets. How wonderful and damning to have both things.

Are my secrets healthy or dead weight? Am I participating in vitality or rushing headlong to demise? Those questions are for the body. How do my secrets, these things of the past, guide me? Am I conscious of their poisons, the toxins I ingest when I remember what I long to forget? Is denial killing me softly with its lullaby, lulling me into inactivity while I wish all the secrets away?

Secrets I have amassed for a lifetime—some mine, some others'. Some leak out when I least expect. Some, I never want to tell. Those eat away at my gut microbiome, destroying my immunity, allowing more invaders in when what I desire is protection—from myself, from the onslaught of their torment.

Secrets drown out the knowing, but my body bears the burden of trauma. Like a heavy weight, it holds memory and secrets...the cries, the torment. Nestled within my adipose cells, secrets absorb and absorb, the fractured, the shattered. My body holds all the dismembered parts of every secret, waiting within, raging within, until I am ready to re-member.

What changes in the body when I say *yes* to participating with Love in the un-wrathing of my secrets?

To divest of the bad stitched into my skin, I must purge the toxins and poisons of my perpetrator's shame, the judgments and actions of another that weigh me down.

I tell myself: Let go. I am safe. Let go. I am here, and I am alive.

When you are safe, let go. Release the tangled mess you have stored within. Move your hand along your belly counterclockwise. Unwind all that has wound you up. Release and let go.

How will you know when it's time? Pay attention to the signals the body offers. And be kind, gentle with your heart, gentle with yourself.

Should I take the scissors and snip away at my secrets, or do they too belong? Are they too a part of the mystery? If I cut at the knotted pieces of thread, won't the whole of it unravel? Is that my desire, to come apart?

Yes. *Yes.* Sophia presses wisdom into my heart. Crowned in resplendent knowledge—of Love, of self, of the cosmos, of ancestry—Sophia guides me to Truth. I can live in the mystery of how all is woven together, even my secrets, like the knotted underbelly that mars a beautiful tapestry. I need not fear the unraveling.

We are dismembered to be re-membered: sifted, refined, and purified in the fire wrought by suffering and tragedy—tragedy not borne of Love, but certainly able to be redeemed by it.

It is a courageous thing to stay in the fire when all I want to do is flee. I anchor my feet to the ground, hand over my heart, and resist the desire to flee from the discomfort of peering into myself and the secrets I need to face.

Because Love is with me, I can face the re-membering with fear *and* curiosity. I do not have to allow my fright to invoke flight. I can stay present to my own discomfort. I can look into myself and face the secrets that are there.

In the Light of Sophia wisdom, I lay my secrets bare on Love's altar. Unrobed, fully disclosed, there in the sanctuary of safety, I watch Love tend my disclosure, handling each shattered, fractured shard with tender mercy and lovingkindness. The breath of Love kisses my painful, traumatic dismembering with Truth. And there, under the banner of Love, I am born anew. Secrets disavowed. Cells restructured. Body reclaimed. The body re-membered.

Secrets that once threatened to pull me under and destroy the weave of my tapestry are integrated like veining. Not cut off and forgotten, as if I have not walked through hell and survived. Sharp edges smoothed by Love. Prickly thorns that once marred the surface are bent. Where the breath once caught and stitched with the inhale of each painful secret, now I can exhale—fully, deeply.

When the blinding pain of secrets gives way, what is left is a mirror, a resonance, a knowing, a freedom. The place of refuge is within, where we can find rest and be re-membered. There, in the solitude of peace, what we've always known to be true will rise to the fore. There, in the absence of the world's slights, in the silence of our secrets' demands and accusations, we can hear, with great clarity, something that rises unbidden from the depth of our being: something imprinted, something knitted into the fabric of our DNA before we were even born. Passed down from Being to being, it was never lost. That is the voice of Love.

Love loves us through and through, even amid secrets that weigh us down. Love invites our participation. Love invites us to re-member. Each body is as human as any other. There is no touch from a master that stops the issue of blood. There is no one to emancipate us from doing our own work of participating with Love. Had the woman not stretched forth her hand to touch his hem, the life energy (*chi/ashé*) that flowed from within Jesus would have never shifted.[35]

With Love's help, cross the chasm. May your soul be anchored in deep, energy-shifting Love. For there, you shall live free.

---

35. See Mark 5:25–34.

I went off to fight the war,
only to discover the war was within.

Feeling inadequate or insecure creates a war within yourself

and often stems from an unhealthy, unconscious comparison

between your actual self (who you are) and your imagined self

(the illusive *you* you think you wanna be).

Do you believe in you—the you that exists

through your achievements, material possessions,

perfect pants size, or projected persona?

What about the stripped down, bare naked you

that only you and the Creator are fully acquainted with?

How content are you with this you?

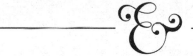

Comparison steals your freedom.

You were meant to live naked

(without pretense, without armor, without the need

to explain or defend) and unashamed.

Every time you measure or compare, you bury a little

of your true self into how someone else does something,

prefers something, or how they live their life.

This is not the death you've been invited into.

Listen for the *sound of the genuine*

within you and say yes to that.

The result of your consent is you

being fully alive and fully free.

Women:

We unconsciously spend our lives as someone else's possession, and when those people or things that so intricately shape the source of our identity no longer exist, we fall apart, unsure of who we are or our place in the world.

We introduce ourselves as so-and-so's wife, daughter, mom, sister, as if the weight of who we are on our own is not enough.

Or perhaps this is a convenient thing that keeps us from doing the work of truly knowing ourselves.

But the question begs some soul searching:

Who are you without the possessive apostrophe of someone else's role and function?

Apart from someone else or something else shaping the framework of your existence, who are you?

Can you, without using a role and function—yours or someone else's—write one sentence about who you are?

Perfectionism is a pillar of patriarchy.

Upon its shoulders rests the lie, "I can control others."

Patriarchy teaches us to: Look the part. Act the part. Be the part.

Just never show up as your truest, most beautiful, fully alive version of yourself, because we don't really want to see or know the real you.

We're satisfied with the quiet, submissive, dolled-up version in her high-heeled shoes and candy-red lipstick.

And we wonder why the world keeps trying to self-improve when she's never been allowed to simply self-accept…

I am me as I am

I am me

I AM!

I keep thinking about Genesis 3:15…

…about the enmity between the serpent and the woman and how the archetypal pattern of those words is living and breathing in our collective society.

For so long, we have lived in a masculine energetic field. Patriarchy and toxic masculinity have ruled the day. Weakness, softness, comfort, compassion, empathy, consolation…all attributes of feminine energy have been pooh-poohed and ridiculed.

For a woman to make it in a *man's world*, she has to *toughen up*, be a b*tch. And yet, where has the overt display of masculine energy gotten us? We are unable to hear one another, competing, comparing, and running roughshod over each other. We are in climate crisis, on the brink of ecological and societal ruin.

Even the earth is groaning for the rise of the feminine. It's not about displacement, replacement, or taking over. This is about balance, harmony…synchronicity.

We have lived the enmity. We have seen the bruised heel and felt the sting of it. Now it's time for us to bruise the head of this *mal* divider, the accuser of humankind.

It's time for the masculine and the feminine to work in concert to heal our land. No longer can we sit by, quietly bearing witness to devastation, and not speak up. We are complicit in our silence.

May it no longer be so. We need both expressions in the fullness of their beauty.

It's time.

People become disillusioned in their pursuit of destiny. Longing and desire have turned into the elusive carrot that always seems within reach but can never be grasped. The chase becomes draining, deafening, defeating. Not allowed the space to be true to our authentic self and voice the weary places of our sojourn, a tug of war ensues between faith-speak and Truth. The heart weeps, longing to be heard, needing to be validated.

We've made purpose and destiny about grandeur and stature: the place I arrive, my measure of achievement or accomplishment. This idea of purpose is ego-driven and self-focused. Our internal preoccupation often leads to a misuse of power and ambition as we strive for placement and notoriety atop a hierarchy.

Destiny happens when I am present to the present moment with the people I am presently with, even if that person is myself. I am living my destiny when I say *yes* to Love in the present moment.

Destiny is doing what we can when we can. It too, like purpose, is more other-centered than me-centered. Douglas Abrams writes, "Purpose, fundamentally, is about how we are able to contribute and be generous to others, how we feel needed by and of value to others."[36]

Purpose and destiny are fueled by generosity. Purpose and destiny are simply saying *yes* to givenness, *kenosis*—the opportunity of self-emptying love.

---

36. Dalai Lama, Desmond Tutu, and Douglas Abrams, *The Book of Joy: Lasting Happiness in a Changing World* (New York: Penguin Random House, 2016), 266.

I used to think of *purpose* as a one-off, fulfilling a singular clarion call, and *destiny* as an achievement, a destination to arrive at, an accomplishment. Then I realized purpose isn't static. My purpose is to incarnate my unique expression of Divine Love, to live fully in my incarnate humanity with clarity and keen awareness. I am to say *yes* each day to participating in Love's dance and to mutually and reciprocally give to others the love I receive in the fellowship of that Knowing.

To that end, destiny is merely weaving with the Master Weaver as I surrender to the mystery of life's journey with all its highs and lows, twists and turns, while participating with Love in *being here now* and expressing that Love in my unique way.

Love longs to bring us all along for the ride. Where will you go in your surrender?

Have you ever stopped to challenge the narrative you've told yourself about your life?

What would it be like to live free, detached from the pictures, demands, and expectations of your illusions?

How much mental anguish are you suffering by measuring your today (your present moment) against a carefully crafted narrative of what you thought success, greatness, winning, achievement (ego terms for "I have arrived") should look like?

If life is a journey, do we ever actually arrive at a fixed destination?

Destiny implies destination. How can we redefine ideas around success to be more in line with an inner state of peace and tranquility?

Rest happens when we live in Love's flow.

Contentment happens when we learn to live in the peace of the mundane spaces of everyday life—alive in the ordinary of our day-to-day.

Quitting something that's not working
requires self-awareness and courage.[37]
— Glennon Doyle

Sometimes, people are afraid to quit, afraid of what others will think, what people will say. Some people equate quitting with failure.

For many, failure is a statement of identity, not a decision or action they own.

For me, quitting is a beautiful *yes, and.*

Yes, I quit, *and* I'm not a failure. I quit because the season for that whatever—job, activity, relationship, group, self-hatred, body shaming, etc.—has run its course. I quit as a recognition that there is no need to hold on to something way past its life cycle, clinging desperately, holding on with resolved attachment, trying to force something or someone to fit where it is not meant to fit.

Yes, I quit, *and* I can own my decision without having to explain it or justify it to anyone else. When quitting is the truest expression of love to myself in this moment, I follow the *yes* of my heart.

Think about it: Why do we allow societal pressure to trap us into pretty boxes when our hearts want out?

Sometimes the courageous thing isn't sticking with something; it's choosing to quit.

---

37. Glennon Doyle, *Carry On, Warrior: The Power of Embracing Your Messy, Beautiful Life* (New York: Simon & Schuster, 2013).

How *do* we know when to stay and when to quit? This is a beautiful part of the dance of life, listening to and being guided by the Inner Knower within our heart.

We don't have to bend the end of our puzzle pieces to try to fit somewhere that is not intended for us.

We will know that place we were meant to fit...it just clicks.

In that place, we can celebrate and love everyone despite our differences. When you land there, don't trade that place for a million yesterdays.

But also know this: Life is a journey. Often, that journey is *yes* until it's *no*.

When the *no* is clear, and the pieces no longer seamlessly fit, it's an invitation to pause, reassess.

We can participate, we can resist change, or we can refuse to acknowledge the invitation to alter our course and tear sh*t up trying to make what's not supposed to work, work.

You're worth more than futile efforts to make crooked fit straight. How many more frayed puzzle pieces are needed before *no* is completely clear?

You get to decide.

What do you love? What are you passionate about? What takes your breath away?

What inspires you? What fills you with awe?

What causes you to throw your head back in utter delight? What brings the sheer joy of tears rushing down your face?

It's easy to get so caught up in the day-to-day of living that the monotony of making do strips away your ability to notice, to be aware.

Noticing is how you begin to participate with Divine Love in givenness.

Your reason for being is the divine dance of mutuality, where you fully own you while giving of yourself in cooperation with the global community for the sake of peace and harmony in our world.

If you're going to resolve anything, resolve to know yourself.

Be aware. Be honest. Be kind.

It's natural, as a human, to resist change until the pain of staying the same becomes greater than the pain of change.

You have to decide what the universe is inviting you into.

Is this growing pain or an invitation to change?

Only you know for yourself what this moment is.

The individual is a microcosm of the whole.

I believe, collectively, we are being invited to change.

What ideals, thoughts, and/or beliefs are we willing to give up, release?

What is the healthiest choice we can make for our society right now?

A CONTEMPLATIVE PRACTICE TO CONSIDER

Naming emotions is one of my most powerful meditative practices. It gives me the freedom to call things out and let them slip through me instead of getting stuck.

I feel guilt, but don't let it turn to shame.

I feel sadness, but don't let it turn to isolation.

I feel anger at God, but don't let that keep me from asking, *Why?*

(After all, I won't get answers unless I am brave enough to ask the questions.)

I feel helplessness, but don't allow myself to stay helpless.

Naming my emotions and allowing them space to move through me creates enough capacity to turn those raw emotions into action and healing, both for myself and others.

We are at a time in history where we are constantly slammed with thousands of negative words and images that affect our emotions, and it's easy to lose faith in all the beauty that humanity embodies.

That beauty and service to one another are where I personally find God.

Friendship *is salvation.*

Community *is salvation.*

And we are all saving each other, one complicated interaction at a time.

My hope, amid catastrophe, is that we would stop tearing each other apart with political, social, and racial differences.

May we go out and look for opportunities where we can co-create through our pain and watch the vapors of beauty and hope *rise up* out of that work.

Are we finally ready?

Love Hard. Be Human. Find Beauty.

In the face of death and war,

everything feels frail, mundane.

And yet I am reminded of Love,

of its beauty, truth, and goodness.

Even as one mourns or suffers,

life is being birthed, lived.

Joy is expanding.

The highs and lows continue

like the top and bottom notes that form a chord

weaving the whole of us together:

Good/Bad

Death/Life

Cheers/Tears

We are all inexplicably bound to one another.

And they came to Bethsaida. And they brought a blind man to Jesus and implored Him to touch him. Taking the blind man by the hand, He brought him out of the village; and after spitting on his eyes and laying His hands on him, He asked him, "Do you see anything?" And he looked up and said, "I see men, for I see them like trees, walking around." Then again He laid His hands on his eyes; and he looked intently and was restored, and began to see everything clearly.
—Mark 8:22–25

T he beauty of community, of friends helping one another, is one of the first things I notice about this biblical passage.

I imagine these friends of the blind man knew they couldn't heal him, but they knew someone who could.

Like these friends, perhaps you aren't the answer to a friend's crisis, their depression, their heartache. Could you refer them to a spiritual director, a trauma-informed therapist, a somatic healer?

This is community shining at its best, that somewhere in the circle of life, someone has answers that bring life and provision—and if they don't, they know somebody who knows somebody who can lead us to someone who can.

Love is the singular dance that weaves and threads its way through multiplicity, through the diversity of community.

We may not have the answer, but we are in Someone who does. The answers don't sit outside, separate from us.

"Yo Jesus, Jesus! This man is blind." Community is a pathway to healing.

My *sangha*[38] is my Girls Nite Out group. We eat together, we drink together. They are my church. They are the place where I lay myself and my life bare. They are the outstretched hands of Jesus, enrobed in flesh, arrayed in varying hues of pigmentation and hair color and texture. Some are mothers, some are not. Some are heterosexual, some are not. Some are married, some are not. Some are Christians, some are not. One is as likely to tell you about the tarot cards she pulled or gift you a crystal as another is to pray for you and give you a prophetic word.

Our table is inclusive, affirming, and accepting. It is a table of freedom, where no one is the others' project for conversion or fixing. It is a table of mutuality and reciprocity. The only supreme thing dominating our table is love.

We have woven a circle where we are free to be, and in that space, we serve as midwives to one another—walking each other toward the source of our being: Divine Love.

GUIDED INQUIRY

Close your eyes or lower your gaze. Take a deep breath: Inhale fully up into your chest. Exhale deeply.

Summon the voice of deep wisdom within you. Ask Spirit: Who is my community? Who are my midwives, my fellow sojourners? Who are the people who will lead me to Love?

Allow their faces to come before you. Offer gratitude for the way you are held in community, for the answers and provision that await within the circle of life.

The second thing I notice about this text is that Jesus takes the man by the hand and leads him away from his village.

---

38. *Sangha* is a Buddhist word for community or a group that comes together for a special purpose.

Why does he do this? Why does he disrupt the man's environment, change his surroundings, take him away to a place that he's not comfortable in, not familiar with?

As a person who is deaf/profoundly hearing-impaired, I am acquainted with the coping mechanisms of the disabled—or differently abled, as some prefer to be called. Blind persons might grab something to hold onto to orient themselves to the place they're in, count steps from the city gate to the shade tree by the road to beg for alms. A deaf/hard of hearing person such as myself would read lips to hear, or use sign language to communicate, or travel with a notepad to ask people to write down what they're saying.

Many people who are differently abled keep things the same. To rely on rote memory as routine is helpful. When the environment is unfamiliar, there's a heightened sense of anxiety or fear—but, and I am speaking purely for myself, it also causes me to be more present in a way that I don't have to be in a familiar environment.

Away from his own village, the blind man doesn't know how many steps he needs to take to get from here to there. He doesn't know where the walls or the ditches are. It's all new. His familiarity has been disrupted. Perhaps, like me, he's more acutely aware of this newness, listening for something familiar to orient himself. I imagine this disruption would feel uncomfortable.

Barbara Brown Taylor once said, "Darkness is a place of unknowing where I'm out of control, where I may be vulnerable to danger, and I may be vulnerable to divine revelation. It is the place where I am least able to protect myself and therefore may be most opened to be transformed."[39]

The great liminal space we are thrust into when we move from knowing to unknowing is dark and vulnerable, but it's also an invitation to transformation if we don't rush past our discomfort.

Comfort is a luxury of the privileged. How has our sense of comfort lulled us to sleep?

---

39. Barbara Brown Taylor, "Don't Be Afraid of the Dark," *Super Soul Conversations with Oprah Winfrey*, podcast audio, August 12, 2018, super-soul.simplecast.com/episodes/barbara-brown-taylor-dont-be-afraid-of-the-dark-QNvvy9ff.

If we allow ourselves to feel discomfort, it will disrupt the status quo. If we stay in discomfort long enough, it will deepen our insight. The tension of discomfort is an invitation into our own growth process.

How is Spirit inviting you outside of your village? Maybe even these ideas of union, inclusion, and participation are outside of your village. What age-old thought processes, belief systems, biblical interpretations, and/or cultural ideologies need to be disrupted? Where are you experiencing the disruption of familiarity?

How many years have you told yourself stories that no longer serve you? How are the narratives of penal substitutionary atonement, eternal conscious torment, and original sin no longer serving you?

Where might Spirit be exposing falsities of things you once believed were true? What whispers has the evil one exalted that need to be made low?

Imagine being ninety and still believing the same things about God, the same things about yourself, the same things about other people, having never accepted Jesus's invitation to take you by the hand and lead you away from your village. What does the evil one continue to repeat that is incongruent with the truth of your being? In what ways has familiarity lulled you into a state of comfort? How has familiarity blinded you, and where are your friends who bring you to Jesus—the midwives, the fellow sojourners who take you by the hand?

Jesus takes the man by the hand, outside his village, outside the temple of the familiar, outside of his normal routine and his everyday place of existence. He disrupts the pattern of movement and leads him in a different direction.

Often, Spirit will lead us out of our comfort zone even as we are being led toward Light, toward still waters, toward the transformative alchemy of wholeness.

Alchemy is not magic. Well, it can be, but I'm referring to the transformation of matter, converting a base metal into gold.

For a follower of the Way, this is an immersion into Love: love transforming us so the core of our existence, the truth of our being, is no longer masked or hidden to us. Our minds are renewed so that we may believe what Love believes about us.

We see in ourselves *big T* Truth: That we are *"fearfully and wonderfully made."*[40] Our dignity is inherent. We and all of creation are in Christ. Our future is hopeful because even it is held in Love. Love validates our worth and deems us rarer than a priceless Monet or van Gogh.

And as Love is shed abroad in our hearts, having its perfect work,[41] we begin to live from that core, from the sound of Love. This is wholeness, where the truth of our being matches the way of our being.

How do we get here? Disruption.

Something has to shift and lead us away from the familiar that is keeping us in a blinded, unconscious state: disruption and Love.

Even with that…I can't help but marvel that in leading the blind man into his own discomfort, Jesus held his hand.

Even in darkness, the light illumines. Jesus grips the man's hand, becomes a support system, a lean-to, a guide. Imagine with me the peace, the utter shalom, that radiates from the person of Jesus as he leads this man. And what of his words? Did Jesus whisper words of comfort in the man's ear?

Jesus holds our hand. We are never alone.

Jesus is shalom. Jesus is comfort. Jesus is Love. Jesus is *for* people.

One day, when I was walking, I felt so clearly that Spirit was asking me to hand over everything I believed to be true about God— every concept, every interpretation, every bit of certainty around my perceived relationship with God—to offer it all to Spirit to sift through and hand back to me what was true. That was more than a

40. Psalm 139:14.
41. cf. Romans 5:5; 1 John 4:17–18; James 1:4.

decade ago. And the crazy thing is, in the self-assured cockiness of a charismatic evangelical, when I gave my wholehearted *yes* to Spirit's invitation, I assumed it would be a one-and-done kind of thing.

Those who are older, wiser, and already have the *been there, done that* T-shirt know that has not played out as I imagined. But Love is a for-real anchor in the stormiest of seas, and in this unraveling of what I was certain was true—my perspectives, my narratives, my projections—there are times I still find myself clinging to some of those. And then there is Love, guiding me by the hand in my blindness and holding on, steady as an anchor.

Jesus guided the blind man outside his village and held on.

GUIDED INQUIRY

I invite you to close your eyes or lower your gaze. Take a deep breath, fully inhaling. Let the breath rise; feel your chest expand. Then exhale. Eyes lowered, listen to the voice of deep wisdom within you.

Ask yourself these questions:

Spirit, what space are you inviting me into that feels disorienting? Where are you trying to disrupt the familiar around me?

Take another breath. What does Spirit say while holding your hand? How do you know that you are being led, being held, being guided?

"Yea, though I walk through the valley of the shadow of death, you are with me. You comfort me. You guide me. You lead me to still waters. You restore my soul."[42]

Jesus held the blind man's hand.

Love, the midwife of our labor;

Love, our fellow sojourner, holds our hand.

---

42. Paraphrase of Psalm 23:1–4.

Jesus spits in the blind man's eyes, then asks, *"Do you see anything?"*[43]

Mark records the blind man as saying: "I can see people, but they look like trees walking about."[44]

Jesus, the one who is life and whose life is the Light of all people, spits in the man's eyes, shining his light into the man's blindness, and the blindness cannot comprehend it.[45]

The man's first gaze after Jesus heals him is to see men like trees walking around.

We only have to stand in the sun to know that light casts shadows, and objects in the shadow appear larger and wider than they really are.

Shadows distort reality.

Bob Mumford once offered these seven Giants.[46] I offer them as allegorical trees I see walking around when I encounter humanity through my first gaze. Perhaps we might consider them as manifestations of our alienation from the truth of our being.

And let me just state, I do not offer this from a haughty place of othering. As Paul Young would say, "These are my people." I have made my home among the trees. With full humility and awareness of the log in my own eye, here are the allegorical trees:

+ The Look Good Tree – beyond external appearance, this tall tree is the shadow of humans creating a reputation that's not established in truth, when the appearance of something is more important than integrity.

+ The Feel Good Tree – this tall tree is the shadow of humans avoiding pain and discomfort at all costs, indulging in excess and compulsive addictive behaviors.

---

43. Mark 8:23.
44. See verse 24.
45. cf. John 1:4–5.
46. Bob Mumford, *Agape Road: Journey to Intimacy with the Father* (Shippensburg, PA: Destiny Image, 2006), chap. 5.

+ The Be Right Tree – this tall tree is the shadow of humans who know everything, humans whose ideas and beliefs are fixed. Humans who are unteachable and have nothing left to learn.

+ The Stay in Control Tree – this tall tree is the shadow of humans who want to determine the outcome of everything for everyone. These humans steer the narrative even if doing so requires manipulation or deception.

+ The Hidden Agenda Tree – this tall tree is the shadow of humans who turn people into projects to save and fix, humans who misuse creation as objects for use and consumption. Like being hit by a snowball with a rock in it, you think you're just hanging out, having fun, and then *wham*! You're blindsided by these humans' unholy intentions.

+ The Personal Advantage Tree – this tall tree is the shadow of humans with selfish ambition and a heady lust for status, jockeying for position.

+ The Remain Undisturbed Tree – this tall tree is the shadow of humans who avoid or manipulate anything that will result in inconvenience or discomfort.

"Discomfort," writes Brené Brown, "is the great deterrent of our generation."[47]

As one that has a high capacity of Enneagram 8 energy, I see these trees all the time. I have an uncanny propensity for spotting injustice and calling people on their bullsh*t.

I see the trees, in myself and certainly in others. So, it's somewhat satisfying to me that Jesus did not deny the shadows existed.

Love does not deny that we have the capacity to act out of our shadow self, to live in ways that are incongruent with the truth of our being. If anyone is wholly acquainted with humanity's wrath and their shadow selves, it's definitely Jesus.

---

47. Brené Brown, *Braving the Wilderness: The Quest for True Belonging and the Courage to Stand Alone* (New York, NY: Penguin Random House, 2017), 152.

Here in the biblical narrative, Jesus does not tell the blind man he was wrong or seeing incorrectly. Nor does he say he has failed, hasn't supernaturally healed the man all the way on the first try. In fact, I almost wonder if the man not seeing correctly is intentional.

Jesus lays his hands on the man's eyes and asks what he sees. "I see men like trees."

Jesus, unbothered, responds: "Yep, that's there. For a time, those I love will walk outside of their name. There will be shadows, projections, egos, false selves. Fig leaves will hide their holy innocence…for a time."

Are the shadows what we see when we live according to our fear instead of with a heart informed by the eyes of Love?

The text tells us, Jesus once again lays his hands over the man's eyes.

The man stared hard. He was restored and saw everything clearly. His second gaze was what Father Richard Rohr calls a long, loving look.

Without seeing, we can't see.

But even with our eyes opened, there are layers to what we see. Do we stop at the trees, at the shadows, or do we sit with Love long enough to see clearly?

There's a diamond waiting to be revealed.

I've been the blind man more than once in my life. After the death of Supreme Court Justice Antonin Scalia, I had a blind moment.

A day or so after his death, I wrote on Facebook:

> Real Talk – Perspective is everything. My news feed has been blowing up with my Christian friends honoring Antonin Scalia and I'm over here struggling, trying not to be mad at a dead man for comments that still feel racially insensitive and devaluing.

This is the man who called the Voting Rights Act "racial entitlement"—the very same man who, two months prior to his death, was in the media for his strongly verbalized opinion that Blacks folks were too slow, not advanced, and unprepared to handle the academic rigor at the University of Texas.

I was flabbergasted by the praise, if not borderline offended. Gently, Spirit blew across my heart:

Don't project the hurt onto your friends because they don't or can't identify with your cultural struggles. I see you. I know you. I intentionally created every tongue, tribe, and nation. Diversity is beautiful to me. I grieve the misunderstandings. But, beloved, you're focusing on the shadow. You see men like trees walking around. Those are the unhealed places of my son that hurt the unhealed places in you, my daughter. And the shadow exists, so I'm not invalidating the pain you feel for those who misunderstand the beauty, strength, and intelligence of your race. But the light of humanity also exists as well. Don't begrudge the people who see his light. Every child of mine was made to shine. Their light, his light, and your light are meant to be celebrated and applauded.

Handing Love my grudge, my offense, Jesus again lays his hands on my eyes.

As the cords that bind me to my negative opinion of Justice Scalia and those who celebrate him are cut, I see everything clearly. And there in the clearing, I am free to release them.

Freedom, love, peace, joy, and celebration of life are all waiting for me as I align my perspective with Love.

In my heart, I've labeled Justice Scalia by his shadow. I've deemed the man a racist not worthy of fanfare. Love deems him a dearly loved son of the Holy Three and celebrates his life.

Breathing in, I release my negative view, ask Spirit to edit the echo of Justice Scalia's slanderous words against my race that keep bouncing off the cavernous space of my heart. I don't want any room for the *"accuser of our brethren"*[48] to keep rehearsing them over and over in my soul.

Generational hurt runs deep and it will wrap us up like a mummy if we allow it.

I admit, I'm a huge work in progress. But I'm learning that being present with my own pain and suffering softens my heart toward the pain of others.

I know the secret history of my own life's sorrow, and Love has taught me how to be kind and gracious toward myself. Taking a second look at my own trees allows me to see the forest and extend that same benevolent compassion.

Noticing is how we begin to participate with Divine Love in givenness. But we can't notice if we can't see.

GUIDED INQUIRY

Where did you first see God's face in another?

Where might Love be inviting you to take a second look?

For every tree, there is also a burning bush: the sacred, holy ground of our inherent dignity. Whose bush is inviting you to turn aside to wonder, to see differently, to pause and remember that we all are holy ground? Where do you need to take off your shoes in reverence?

Whom have you discarded without a second look?

I can observe once, see people like trees walking around, and be informed by this shadowed perception, or I can intentionally participate with the flow of Love, fix my gaze on the eyes of Love, and be transformed to see clearly.

May we gaze beyond the trees to the Light of humanity.

May the light within us ripen to self-giving love.

---

48. Revelation 12:10.

May we see one another with clear eyes.

May we embrace one another with clear hearts,

for we all are burning bushes on the path home to Love.

Inside this passage in Mark 8, I find myself working on my heart to move from seeing people like trees to embracing that second gaze, the long, loving look where I see clearly.

I have a sense that when the eyes are clear, the whole body is full of light. From that place, I offer this earnest aspiration:

> Dearest Love, even when I see the pain of another expressing itself through character defects and shadows, help me have space in my heart to hold them with compassion. And to the best of my own emotional capacity, form my heart to care about their suffering.

I see people like trees, and I know you do not begrudge me when that is what I see. But I remember the words of Henry Wadsworth Longfellow: "If we could read the secret history of our enemies, we should find in each man's life sorrow and suffering enough to disarm all hostility."[49] So lay your hands on my eyes once more, that I might see clearly.

49. Henry Wadsworth Longfellow, "Drift Wood, A Collection of Essays: Table-Talk," *Prose Works of Henry Wadsworth Longfellow*, 1857.

Long before he laid down earth's foundations, he had us in
mind, had settled on us as the focus of his love, to be made
whole and holy by his love.
—Ephesians 1:4 MSG

Fear of man – that moment when the appearance of something is more important than someone. Without authenticity, vulnerability, and transparency, we will continue to foster disconnection and false intimacy in relationships.

O LORD, who may abide in Your tent? Who may dwell on Your holy hill? He who walks with integrity, and works righteousness, and speaks truth in his heart. (Psalm 15:1–2)

Fear of man – when saving face is more important than telling the truth.

In the face of fear, these are the choices that create opportunities for Love to be fully formed in me:

- I will not perform for love. Being known through relational connection trumps being known for what I do.
- I will not be a part of something where the appearance of something is more important than the something. Vulnerability and transparency matter more than what people think.

- I will not elevate right behavior over a right heart. Behavior modification without heart change creates actors, not transformed people.

- I will not be motivated by fear. I will look to see where Love is leading and follow.

IMPORTANT DISTINCTIONS

Jesus says, "I do nothing of myself,"

not

"I am nothing."

Jesus says, "I and the Father are one,"

not

"I am the Father."

You are a living, breathing human being made in the image of God.

You are worthy.

You are valuable.

It is a lie to say you are no-thing when you were created and called not only good, but very good.

Remember who you are.

Remember the Source of your own becoming.

I believe firmly in going to your fellow human if they wronged you. I believe in confrontation. I believe in brave communication. But I do not believe in or support the *fear of man*[50] in any form.

Anytime the appearance of something, or how something appears to another, becomes more important than people and relational equity, to the point that you manipulate and control who I tell or what I say or you have to give me the story you want told "so we're all on the same page," we're bordering on a cult.

Love never asks us to sacrifice our voice or our unique personhood to tow the party line. And for sure, the Divine ain't no mob boss.

The banqueting table is for everyone. It's not us, the supposed family of God, versus them, the world.

Nothing about Love is rooted in the lie of separation.

It's time out for Jim Jonesing our way through life without even pausing to think or question for ourselves.

If you're being abused, run like hell.

I don't care if it's spiritual abuse, verbal abuse, physical abuse, or mental abuse—it does *not* matter. Leave the sunken space and get out.

And if you want to tell or talk about it, go ahead and sing like a canary. Maybe you'll save someone else from the mind warp in the process.

---

50. "Fear of man" is charismatic Christianese. I opted to leave the idiom intact rather than change it to something more inclusive to highlight its patriarchal subtleties.

I know I don't know all there is to know about God, but I'm gonna stake my life on this: Jesus is a whole lot freer than most of the conditions and constraints we try to bind people up in because of our own personal preferences and constraints.

Secondly, God really isn't as angry and punitive as we want the Holy Three to be. The Divine has a vast amount of respect and unconditional love for humanity.

The most freeing thing you can do for yourself is to give people the space to walk out their own unique journey. They aren't you.

Trust Divine Love.

The Holy Three found you. The Holy Three changed you. The Holy Three speaks to you. The Holy Three leads you.

Isn't the Divine big enough to do that for others without us having to police people?

At some point, we're gonna need to take a hard step back from the hoodwinking and colonizing and examine afresh the ways, whys, and motives behind some of the ideology we've been handed in *form* (enslaver, colonizing, white supremacist, patriarchal Christianity), with no *power*[51] (love), and unravel the untruths from the person of Christ, who predates co-opting and whitewashing.

To be sure, there are beautiful parts of the Trinity and the Way of Love which we are to emulate and embody.

But there are also some narratives it's past time for us to discard.

May Spirit shine a light on what we may not even know we're ready to see.

---

51. cf. 2 Timothy 3:5.

I am a product of the church. I have been churched for most of my life. Even when I hate it and want to divorce myself from it, I find it in the sinew of my tendons, oozing from the marrow of my bones, so much so that if you ask what comes to mind when you say "wilderness," up from my pores comes, *"Then Jesus was led up by the Spirit into the wilderness to be tempted by the devil."*[52]

In the face of prestige, position, and power, the wilderness evokes every fear of isolation, aloneness, and scarcity. How does one survive in uninhabited terrain outside of capitalism, hospitality, and socialization? What does one do in a foreign place, on foreign soil, when they have not yet cultivated life?

For some, the wilderness is their rites of passage. Ready to face apartness, to overcome egoic ambition and self-preservation, they turn inward. Solitude creates a well of spaciousness to step into their largeness. They are prepared to own their true self, to see with clarity the way they are to live and move and have their being, crystalizing the way they orient themselves in the world.

I see this in the Matthew 4 passage with the wisdom teacher Jesus. He understood himself and what was at stake. And even in the dry, parched desert, he withstood the desperation that scarcity breeds.

The tempter had invented imaginings, spun plausible what-ifs to validate self-protection over trust. But Jesus had a clear vision of Love and how he was to live and move and orient himself in response to Love.

---

52. Matthew 4:1.

As tempting as the tempter can be, spinning all kinds of harrowing webs to lure us into darkness, what if the wilderness is the place of our own hero's journey, the place of solitude where we connect to the parts of us that remember where and how and from whence we come?

Instead of torment that churns a myriad of narratives to justify our selfishness, what if the barren landscape of our wilderness is an invitation for us to sit with, be with, allow, accept, yield, and surrender?

Forty days and forty nights, Jesus found himself in the wilderness, and not until the end did the angels arrive to minister to him. What sustained him in this barren place? How could he be so resolute in his knowing? I refuse to offer platitudes or best guesses dressed up as certainty. The truth is, I don't know.

What I do know is that the wilderness is filled with disorientation. It balloons like a child's soapy bubble filled with the shitty first draft of a narrative designed to trap us in despair.

In the unknown, fear plays its fiddle.

Stop.

Close your eyes and breathe deeply.

What does fear feel like in you? Are you aware of the shape of your fear? What is its shape, its story?

Where is fear trapped in your body?

Do you recognize its sensations?

What web does fear weave around you?

Do you take the ride into hell (torment), or do you acclimate to the unknown, to get used to new ways of knowing?

As harrowing as the wilderness is, when you yield and embrace the journey, it is possible to find peace.

What of the wilderness evokes a sense of gratitude? Where do you sense abundance in the wilderness? Are you able to intuit places of congruence even in the wilderness?

Acknowledgment of both desolation and consolation is one of the ways love is formed within.

In the wilderness, you can panic or you can choose to receive Love into every part of you. You can trust Love to be your bulwark, to hold you as you unravel, to keep you safe in liminality, to ground you even as you face the mysteries of life. In the wilderness, there is an opportunity to learn that fear is not the opposite of Love.

Love has no opposite. Love is strong enough to hold all things, even your fears. Love is not afraid of your wrestle, your anger, or your disappointment. Love does not ask you to hide big mad or your questions or angst. Love is strong enough to withstand the ferocity of your heart's desert storms. Love knows those things are invitations to your evolution and transformation.

Know this for sure, even in the wilderness: Love is in the middle of everything you perceive to be barren and desolate, working it for your good. If the wilderness teaches you anything, let it teach you that there are treasures in the desert.

The solitude of the wilderness teaches you to value the moment in front of you. To love this day, this place, before you fully know it. To trust that as the mysteries unfold, Love will attend to your good. And, even in suffering, Love offers comfort. There is no glossy-eyed oasis in the middle of the desert.

And yet, the invitation remains the same: to heal and to embody Love in the rockiest isolated terrain.

What if the wilderness is more about your transformation than the tempter's temptation?

Can I be honest? I have never really liked church. I became a Christian solely because of the idea of hell.

The best thing that ever happened to me was encountering Love and dispelling the myth of eternal conscious torment.

I think most preachers mean well, but most Black preachers in particular are still regurgitating the ideas of an enslaver's God who is retributive, punitive, to be feared, far off, demanding of servitude, and transactional.

Once I realized it was these ideas and interpretations of God that I didn't necessarily like, I was able to lay a foundation of relationship built on Love and Truth that was more Spirit-led than fear based.

One of my biggest preacher struggles is standing above people, talking at them instead of talking with them. If this is the table where we break ourselves open and pour ourselves out, why am I the only dish being served?

How do we truly commune as a body and invite people into a conversation on Sunday morning without just espousing a bunch of ideas and interpretations that make us look and sound smart? What if we started flipping the script on this thing?

What are you thinking about? What are you pondering? How does the text, the Christian experience, come alive in you?

For years, I sat in church—the preacher or the preacher's wife, whichever moniker people can swallow—reading books stuck inside my Bible because my heart was screaming, "Does that even make sense? Well, what about…? There has to be more!"

I'm grateful we're getting free enough to challenge things out loud, to wrestle through, to be okay with not reaching a resolution, to sit with not knowing instead of creating an explanation. But every time I grace a pulpit, I just want to have a mic on the side, sit down on the stairs, and say, "Let's talk about it."

Show up *with* me; don't show up *for* me. Everything in me that's pedestal-worthy exists in you too.

Tribalism and groupthink scares the bejeebers out of me. I've seen the wake of their damage and destruction too many times in my small existence on the planet—so much so that I'm completely okay hanging out at the margins observing, pondering, wondering, and wandering.

I can see you and celebrate you without having to parrot you or buy the company T-shirt.

When *all in* means I lose the ability to think for myself and ask questions, I might need to pause and ask myself, "Is this really healthy?"

When *all in* means I'm relegated to silence when I call foul or challenge a decision, I might need to pause and ask myself, "Is this really healthy?"

I'm not advocating questioning everything with skepticism. I'm advocating being in community where we are free to be our most authentic self, where the value of who we are is significant.

When I'm only as good as my usefulness or my ability to allow my gifts to be consumed, I might need to pause and ask myself, "Is this really healthy?"

Wonder and mystery keep my heart open to Love and to believing the best about people.

How do you feel in your community? Are you alive and energized? Are you always having to be careful about how you form what you say? Are you seen and known? After you've invested hours of your time, energy, and resources, do you feel there is a valuable return on your investment?

Too often, we go numbly through our lives, not checking in with our hearts.

You don't have to settle for the next rote thing. You can say *yes* to the next alive thing.

Where is the place and who are the people that energize you and make you come alive?

Find that place. Discover those people. Build friendships.

Enjoy community, but don't ever sacrifice your own mind to be a part of the tribe.

When the chants of "We Are Something" overpower the song of "I AM," you might want to pause and ask yourself, "Is this really healthy?"

Be YOU.

When reimagining darkness as something other than evil, I don't have a problem with God being light, or that in the Holy Three, there is no shifting shadow. The problem comes when light is associated with whiteness and purity, and everything dark is associated with evil, bad, demonic, and impure. From the negative psychological connotation of our *shadow* to the theological baggage that was woven into our present-day psyche from Cotton Mather's two grandfathers and beyond, we must acknowledge the way our dualities and our literal interpretation of the creation narrative have driven our conscious and unconscious biases. Barbara Holmes speaks to this: "The disassociation with darkness as the price of assimilation has alienated dark people from its restorative potential."[53]

Perhaps we might consider reframing, or at the very least recognizing, the luminous darkness and the presence of Spirit hovering even there.

Many interpret the narrative as beginning with darkness as void, formless, and then moving to form when light was separated from darkness, and a clear divide made. I wonder, though, if in our desire to cut off bad from good, we've splintered Love's intent for wholeness. Perhaps this delineation speaks to the cyclical nature of disorder/order/reorder/disorder, not as a one-time event but simply a rhythm like the seasons. If so, we might be able to redeem our catastrophic experiences and faith deconstructions instead of trying to cut them off completely.

How is the Spirit brooding over your dark spaces? What is being formed in your disorder? How can you hold and relax into periods of darkness without being afraid or viewing them as *bad*?

53. Barbara A. Holmes, *Joy Unspeakable: Contemplative Practices of the Black Church*, 2nd ed. (Minneapolis, MN: Fortress Press, 2017), 8.

The way the soul walks to God is through
human unknowing.
—St. John of the Cross

What if *deconstruction* is really humans shedding all the ways we have come to perceive and know God through the finite capacity of our human limitations?

What if what people are really deconstructing is an unhealthy, toxic version of a punitive, uncaring, uninvolved God?

If eternal life, as Jesus said in the Gospels, is truly knowing the Father and the one He sent, what if *deconstruction* is simply moving from a form, detaching from familiarity—what we think we know about God—to knowing the expansiveness of who God actually is?

Love is fully committed to freeing us from every bond that blinds us from Truth. We make dirty words out of everything we don't understand when Love is merely inviting us into transformation.

There was a time when I didn't read books from other religions or engage with wisdom teachers from other faith traditions. I'd been taught to be wary of being deceived by a *spirit of error* and that even the *elect* could be led astray. I was told that I'd be confused by opening myself up to these *demon-possessed people*—because, in my faith tradition, anyone who didn't believe, confess, or practice exactly as we did, with the exception of maybe Judaism, since we co-opt several of their practices—were clearly going to hell and not of God.

Later, I realized that was more brainwashing from colonized Christianity to keep people silent, in check, and disengaged from critical thinking, rather than embracing the wide, inclusive belonging of the cosmic Christ.

So I started reading broadly, across faith traditions, finding their wisdom teachers to be companions on the Way along with other wisdom teachers within my own faith tradition. Today, I honor the place in my own journey that allows me to trust Divine Love and Spirit as they lead me into *all* truth, not just someone else's interpretation of truth.

I'm a deeply spiritual person who has embraced practices of interspirituality in my communion with Divine Love.

I very much hold as an anchor certain tenets of my Christian faith, but can I be honest? Going to church is not a golden calf; it is not the cure-all to every issue and character defect we face.

And that's not to negate church attendance either, but when our answer to every woe and problem is, "They need to be in church," we need to be honest about how we've made church attendance a savior instead of Jesus.

Where church is healing for some, it's traumatic for others.

Where church is community for some, it's isolation for others.

Where church is an escape and *the answer* for some, it's not for others.

Life is not reductionistic.

Love will play the song for you in your key.

Pause. Listen to your heart. Trust Spirit to guide you into all truth.

If nature is church for you, let nature be the place you commune.

If the four walls of a building with praise dancers and a preacher is church for you, let the building be church for you.

We've got to stop forcing and projecting our reality, our way of communing, onto others.

It drives people away from Love, when the only way forward is toward.

I traded dreaming big and my belief in a prophetic destiny for being present and living intentionally with Love as life unfolds. Even in that, there are things that speak to my heart, places that call to me.

Color is one such thing. The more riotous, bold, and vivid the color, the louder its resonance echoes within me.

Art calls to me. It grounds me, settles me, connects me to the world around and within me in a way that only the ocean can surpass.

When I lost the ambition to become something for others to consume and objectify, my life slowed.

In the absence of longing to be famous, to make something, do something grand, and/or create a platform and a full itinerary, competition and comparison subside.

I know, false humility won't allow us to truthfully admit we judge ourselves by our accomplishments or lack thereof. Pride won't allow us to confess that we struggle with any of these things—the longing, the need, the greed, the desire.

Until, one day, my heart just decided—what if I pulled back from the race and allowed myself to find myself within myself? What if I allowed myself to believe what the Divine believes and allow that to be enough? What if I achieve nothing more than waking up each day and loving me?

What if I traded striving for a far-off future prophetic destiny for an awakened today, to fully live in the present moment?

May the fulfillment of quiet longings, desired places to see and behold, remind you that you don't have to make a trade. You can make a culmination.

You can still dream and tuck your desires for tomorrow away in your heart. And you can still be awake, present in this moment.

For when the two collide, it's a riotous display of living color.

Moving into contemplative, mystical, *enlightened* spaces, I find myself grappling with people who promote nothingness or no-thing as the ultimate point of transcendence.

It confuses the heck out of me, given all the beautiful diversity we can see and identify with, subject to subject, amongst the trees, the flowers, the birds, etc.

But when it comes to diversity and uniqueness of personhood, I'm supposed to want to leave my God-given Blackness and meld into the nothingness of *pure light*.

I'm not sure if I'm more bothered by the fact that these ideals are mainly taught by people with little to no melanin, who don't have far to go to get to the nothingness of *pure light*, or the fact that *pure light* is considered something more worthy to ascribe to than, say, the luminous darkness of the cosmos.

Perhaps both/and…but that's my internal daily, sometimes hourly, wrestle.

We all seem to be struggling with the different ways in which dominance masquerades as righteousness.

People talk about church hurt, and it's true. The *church* doesn't hurt people; people in the church hurt people. Church leaders hurt people. People in whom you put your trust and faith and hope hurt people. People you have believed the best about and given up your very life to support will hurt people.

And who is the *church*, if not the people?

We shy away from the responsibility of dealing with our broken places and the inner wounded child in all of us that leads to cycles of perpetuating hurt.

In July of 2013, I walked away from the church—not the Trinity or Their people, just the institution. Then Doug and I moved into the heart of the city, and we wanted to participate in the community of Atlanta that was committed to change. Being conditioned church groupies, the only way we knew to do that was through the church. And we tried several.

Through a series of divine interventions, in 2015, we landed at St. Luke's Episcopal Church. St. Luke's, named for the apostle who was also a physician. St. Luke's, the Episcopal church that offers healing prayers each Sunday.

It's hardly coincidental that St. Luke's, the church of refuge with their healing prayers, would play a role in my healing journey. Hands down, the Episcopal diocese in Atlanta is hugely responsible for restoring my faith and belief in the *church*.

Am I still walking with a limp all these years later? Absolutely.

Touch the right tender spot, and it will set me off on a bad church rant. But I know, without a shadow of a doubt, devoid of a revelation of Divine Love to keep me rooted in the Holy Three, I could have easily become an atheist.

If you have not walked through the depth of pain one experiences when their Tower of Babel comes crashing down, don't judge their outrage. And for those who have fallen from the ivory tower or been pushed off because someone in the church hurt you, know there is indeed a balm that heals all wounds.

Your faith in the institution may never be restored, as St. Luke's did for me, and that's okay.

But the very One who is Love sees all things and holds you in the palm of Love's hand.

It's okay to be angry. We need to feel that betrayal, the loss, the death of our belief in an ideal. Process that anger in a safe space. Don't spew it, and don't let it fester on the inside, or you will become embittered. And when you're bitter, you can lose faith in the world and the people around you.

Here's to the churches that are less like cults and more like institutions of hope.

Here's to the churches that aren't pretending to have all the answers while turning their backs to injustice.

Here's to the churches that don't declare "Kingdom now" but live the Love of God every day.

Here's to the churches that don't make a project of people or use them as tools for their consumption.

Here's to the churches that see the glory of the Divine in every living soul without needing to post Facebook testimonies of their *spoils* or endeavors to help the lowly.

'Tis true what they say: One bad apple doesn't spoil the whole bunch.

Let me tell y'all what's hypocritical AF:

Folk who go to church on Sunday and worship the King of the Jews while supporting the self-proclaimed king of the Jew.

Voting for and supporting national welfare by giving billions of dollars to a country each year while whining and complaining that universal healthcare or free tuition for college is excessive and exorbitant.

Yet the aforementioned, unnamed small country, with our government handout bankrolling them, offers both universal healthcare *and* free college to their citizens—all while small business owners in our country can't afford healthcare or maintain their businesses in the face of dire illness.

We are either woefully uninformed as a people

or intentionally turning a blind eye.

And yes, I feel some kind of way about it.

My question is: Why don't you?

I've had too much time in the game. I've seen the highs of being in church leadership and—trust me—I've seen the lows. I've seen the bodies used, consumed, and discarded. I've seen rejection. I've seen verbal and spiritual abuse. I've seen words twisted like sea monsters to rob people of their worth, as if we could slip inherent dignity off like a wetsuit. But I've watched senior leaders do it and call it love or *mentoring*.

And please, don't come for this momma bear on this church thing. Imma tell you right now, I got all the feels about it. Too many people have been hurt, and their pain discarded and discounted by those who are still deeply enmeshed in church life.

And it's okay to be in church, sold out…whatever, whatever. We need all kinds. I'm not knocking where you are on your walk.

But I am gonna say, it's inconsistent AF to have theological beliefs that allow you to treat people like refuse. No Scripture, no interpretation of Scripture, ever makes it okay to step over another's consent.

The shepherd left ninety-nine sheep for the lost one. And just because a coin is *lost* does not mean the value of that coin has diminished.[54]

People matter.

More than credo, more than our ragtag, tacked together, flimsily held beliefs—which will change as we change and grow and evolve—people matter.

---

54. See Luke 15:4; 15:8.

Love God, yes. Eternal life is to know God and the One He sent.[55]

I'm here for the knowing: the deep, intimate knowing; the relational, abiding, transformative knowing. And I'm also here for the second part of the commandment: Love people.

Anytime I exalt what I believe or feel called to protect my religion above people, there's a problem. If we cannot or will not stop for the one, sit with them in their pain and suffering, acknowledge the harm, trauma and/or abuse they have suffered, we have a problem.

We are clinging too tightly to labels, to religious identification, rather than to the Way of Jesus.

May it cease to be that our loyalties lie more in our identification to a faith tradition than in caring for the hearts of people.

---

55. See John 17:3.

Sometimes we as a people can get so hoodwinked by the oppressive tenets of church doctrine and fear that we don't know how to live in freedom.

Some people have been spouting bad/incorrect theology for so long, repeating things that have been passed down to them, and it's easy to glibly trust people because they stand in elevated positions.

But please don't check your brain at the door.

"It is for freedom that you've been set free. Don't return again to a yoke of bondage."[56]

This invitation from the apostle Paul is true, whether we are leaving oppressive things of *the world* that have hindered us from living into the truest expression of ourselves; or oppressive teachings of *the church* that restrict us from living our truest, fullest expression of our humanity; or oppressive teachings that cause us to judge others who may be living their fullest, truest expression of their humanity in a way we wouldn't necessarily live ours.

Be wise.

Be true to Love.

Be boundaried, yes,

but allow Love to be the structure that governs your freedom.

---

56. See Galatians 5:1.

People are in process.

It's not our job to be the theology police as they walk through their unique-to-them journey with Love.

When invited and given access to others:

share your opinion,

offer wisdom,

but more than anything,

take their hand,

place it in Wisdom's hand,

then pull your hand back.

Encourage them to hear what Love is saying to them.

Come alongside.

Help people get rid of their sea legs.

Companion, bear witness

until they can stand in the strength of their own love, peace, and hope.

I think often of how a Christian hermeneutic that has us rapture-focused and shunning our bodies—the flesh is weak, the flesh is evil, subdue the flesh, etc.—has left us largely disconnected from our lived reality.

I'm amazed at the amount of environmental waste and lack of concern for the climate or the citizens who occupy our planet—really, for anyone who isn't professing Jesus and singing revival songs. And I often wonder how much of that is because the American evangelical church has been stuck in the time warp of *the last days* and a soon-to-come rapturing Jesus who will whisk us all away.

Besides, if I'm not planning to be around, then I don't have to own my part in showing up as a concerned or actively involved citizen—unless it means stopping someone I feel is infringing upon my idea of freedom: the right to bear any arms I want, the right to be Christian, the right for America to *only* be Christian, the right to be heterosexual, and the right to add to this list at will.

Somehow, we only think about voting en masse for a presidential election (but never local elections) and only then to protect the rights of the unborn, and damn all the humans who actually are alive and couldn't manage to pull themselves up by their bootstraps or be saved from their economic position through prayer and fasting.

We need more than a theology that excuses us from showing up while we wait to check out.

We keep trying to learn how to be Christians with our heads. Never mind that *Christian* was once a derogatory slur used to mock followers of the Way.

Like picking up a manual or studying for a test, we learn the latest formula to pray or Scripture to recite. We become well versed in strategy, and our heads get it…they really do.

But it's in the heart that all wars are won. It's in the heart that transformation happens.

It's in the connecting of our hearts to Love and to one another that we can truly begin to grasp what it means to live an abundant life of freedom.

Freedom is not obtained in our heads. Love is not experienced in what we know. It's received in our hearts and emptied out through the gut, our seat of compassion.

When my heart is captured, I'm all in.

And in the safety of Divine Love, I give out. ("Out of your belly shall flow rivers of living water.")[57]

Like the kinetic energy of a waterwheel, filling, emptying, moving in sync to the hum of the water, the grace to be, to change, and to transform comes when we allow ourselves to relax and give in to the flow.

We never obtain the beauty of the dance when counting the steps in our heads.

---

57. See John 7:38.

At some point, we have to close our eyes, become one with the music, and trust our bodies to find their rhythm.

Recognize the invitation that lingers: the *yes, and* of life.

It's not head over heart *or* head or heart.

It's head, heart, gut—every part has been invited to show up in this transformation process.

Will you say *yes?*

> *We think we authored God, rather than realizing*
> *He authored us.*
> —Marianne Williamson

Rather than believe humanity is filled with loving human beings whom God created, we've taken the dysfunctional bleakness that lies within the alienated, untransformed heart and projected that onto the character and nature of God.

We are angry, judgmental, and schizophrenic in our behavior, and we hold up these attributes and say, "Look, here is God. God does indeed get angry. God does indeed judge."

But what if...the judgment of the Holy Three is Their love?

What if Love is coming on the scene to harmonize the misaligned?

And maybe, just maybe, the Holy Three is indeed angry...at everything that alienates, that stands in the way of us receiving Their love and being transformed by it.

Who's to say?

Rather than try to be an authority on God, I'd much rather believe that Love's grace is indeed sufficient for me.

I'd rather come into complete agreement with what Love sees and what Love says about me.

At the core of each human being is Love.

Like a treasure hunt, sometimes it requires digging through a whole lot of wet, slogging mud to discover the gold—but it's there.

I promise, it's there.

One day, I found myself grumbling, "Christianity is supposed to be about family living in relationship with you, Jesus, and Spirit, in the place you've made for us—in your house. Yet so many have made it a place where orphans are trying to rise to the top of the hierarchy in the orphanage."

And gently, Love spoke to me, "Beloved, don't despise the journey of others. You can never fully understand the path of another unless you've walked it. Only I journey the path of all my beloveds."

The Beloved's compassion and respect for people absolutely astound me.

Humbly, I hand Love my frustration and recalibrate my heart to align with the Holy Three.

All roots need deep, dark, earthy places to create life above the surface.

Prayers root us to the Divine.

Effectual prayer is living inside the energy and quality of relationship with Love. When we live in the flow of Love, we pray.

Prayer is our *"may it be done to me"*[58]—the place of mutuality and trust, the place where Love surrenders to love and love surrenders to Love: *"Into your hands I commit my spirit."*[59]

Prayer is more than list making, asking, or beseeching.

Prayer is breathing.

Prayer is being.

Prayer is the awareness of Divine Love in our life.

Prayer is being present.

Prayer is awe.

Devoid of the voices that propel us deeper into insanity, may we wake up and live into the truth of our being. May our hearts be at home with our *be*-ing. May the mystery of at-*one*-ment and the intimate immediacy of Love bring us to a place of peace.

---

58. Luke 1:38.
59. Luke 23:46.

God has always loved...the Son, you, me, the world, creation. The whole of our existence is based on relationship.

And yet, somehow along the way, consciously or unconsciously, we began to exalt consumption and transaction above relationship.

This is evident in our obsession with God *using* someone and our willingness to *be used* by God.

God, who delights in you, has no desire to *use* you. The Holy Three has no desire to use anyone to bring about some sense of cosmic justice.

God, who is wholly relational, submits in love and defers to us. The Holy Three delights in participating in our lives with us. And loves it when our eyes are opened to the truth of union—that the Divine is not a far-off God on a faraway throne, but is in us, with us, alongside us.

The joy of living relationally with the Holy Three is that we get to receive from Love, and Love gets to receive from us. And the more we are convinced of the Divine's love, the more of ourselves we freely give and entrust to the Holy Three.

It's a dance, not a transaction.

We are the people of the Holy Three, dearly loved ones, not tools.

This wrong belief is why we so easily and freely use people for their gifts and calling. We attempt to drain every bit of life from others in the name of...something.

This is a false image of God, and it causes us to devalue people.

The Holy Three's respect, love, honor, value, and delight for you as Love's own is too great for you to reduce yourself or allow yourself to be reduced to a tool.

You can't have a relationship with a tool.

Tools perform. People commune.

The sun beams. The grass beckons. I heed its welcome and lay on my back, bare feet to the earth, knees upright to support my frame. Shielding my eyes, I stare at the sky, naming each majestic cloud as an image I've formed in my mind's eye. *Horse. Chicken leg. Heart.* I think about clouds as images, clouds as covering. And somehow, I think about God.

Where is God in the clouds? How do I name that which I've deified? How cloudy are my images of God? What or who do I imagine God to be?

Tradition has given me some answers. Many words have been written to substantiate humanity's beliefs about God. I've parroted a lot of them. But how do we truly begin to know God in that passionate, deep, mystical, unveiled knowing that Jesus speaks of in John 17:3: "*This is eternal life, that they may know You, the only true God, and Jesus Christ whom You have sent*"?

The god of my childhood was a god who "whooped up on your head" to get you to do what he wanted you to do (which is utter manipulation, by the way), the god who caused bad things to happen if you didn't tithe or prioritize church attendance, the god who condemned people to eternal conscious torment (hell) if you didn't repeat the sinner's prayer, a god who was literally coming back on a white horse at

Armageddon to kill people. This god was not good. This god was an aberration of the stories we tell ourselves to weave some semblance of certainty out of mystery and a projection of our own delusion when we are alienated from Love. But it was the god that was woven into the fabric of my life through someone else's theology.

How do we unravel someone else's ideas from the truth of who God is?

Great Spirit of Love, show us where to begin. Reveal to us what is Truth and strip away all that we have created in your image and likeness that does not serve you or our relationship with you.

May we have eyes to see where we, or others we admire, have ascribed bad things to your nature to explain away our pain. May we be able to distinguish between theologies birthed in suffering and the truth of who you are. May we be able to identify where we've sated ourselves with certainty when you were inviting us into mystery. May we come to know you as good, and only good, and experience the depth of your Divine Love as healing, regenerative, and transformative.

If what we believe to be true about God frames every part of our existence, whose inherited ideas have shaped the foundation of our God concept? What preconceived notions or habits of thought might we be projecting onto God? Are those preconceptions our own? How did we arrive at those conclusions? If what we believe about God frames our lived experience and how we relate to and interact with the world around us, how are we discovering or rediscovering Divine Love for ourselves?

How might Divine Love be inviting us to reorient our mind to the Holy Three's goodness and kind intentions toward us?

For the greater part of my life, I lived with a superficial, shallow god who was angry, distant, and always waited until "late in the midnight hour" to turn things around—or didn't, using bad events to teach me a lesson. Like the clouds I imagined were horses, hearts, and chicken legs, I remade god into an undependable, unfeeling, callous,

Zeus-like image, more devil than deity—just white and big instead of red with a tail and pitchfork. Vision clouded, disappointment kept me from knowing Divine Love and seeing Love as Love truly is.

One day, I met a couple who described God as a Father who loves me, a Mother who comforts and welcomes me and prepares a seat for me at her bountiful table. They described a God who was running toward me and not from me, a God who wasn't withholding good from me because I forgot to pay my tithes, a God who included and affirmed *all*, whose banner over *all* is Love.

The core of my being leaped, inviting me to challenge all that I once believed to be true about God. Like the clouds above, could I have imagined an illusion, an image of God that wasn't exactly there? Was my mind playing tricks on me? Had I conjured a false, graven image of God?

Indeed…I had.

Thankfully, I'm seeing a bit clearer now. I've since come to know this God, this nonbinary expression of Divine Love; this generous, compassionate One; this God who lives among us and in us, even when we are completely unaware of the Divine's presence within us. This is the God who loves us with an everlasting love.

God is in our midst, a God who exults over us with joy, who quiets us in love, who rejoices over us with shouts of joy and gathers those who grieve.[60]

But how do we get to the place where this is the God we see, the God we encounter and know, the God who frames our imaginings when we think of God?

Stillness, perhaps. Contemplative prayer, maybe.

For me, Divine Love is unveiled through communion, connection, and acts of living that create openhearted wonder.

Consistent engagement with spiritual practices often invites us into such spaciousness, creating access points for us to become

60. See Zephaniah 3:17–18.

more consciously aware of Divine Love's kenotic expression in us and through us.

To that end, all spiritual practices have this purpose—to allow us to touch the depths of our inner selves and to live a generous life of participation with Divine Love in absolute openheartedness; to move from what we know in our heads about God to living and moving and having our being in God; to be present in this life, to the world around us, and to Divine Love.

What is true about God? *God is Love.*[61]

The experience of Love loving us allows us to feel and then to see. As Love invades our numbed-out parts, awakening us from cloudy misperception to Truth, we are invited to heal and to believe what Love believes about us, to trust in the benevolence and kind intentions of Love. Trust flourishes in the soil of Love. And there, our God image transforms.

We don't just decide to see God as loving; Love is who God is. To encounter Divine Love is to encounter our deepest self.

We are the *imago Dei,* the image of God, the embodiment of Love existing in interior freedom, uniquely expressing its beauty, truth, and goodness to the external world around us.

May we gaze in the clouds and experience the wonder of Divine Love loving us.

61. See 1 John 4:16.

We are all intricately interwoven, supported by, and held in Love.

May we all have each other's backs more than fighting over words.

May we be consciously aware of our connection to Joyful Presence.

May we feel supported and held by each other, by the universe, by Divine Love.

And don't @ me about the *universe*. Love hovered over it just as Love hovered over us.

Love dances over the cosmos just as Love dances and delights over us.

We can't be free while carrying socialized conditions of the world or any other person's ideas and expectations about a thing.

We have to get still and quiet enough to be re-membered—all of our pieces, parts, and fragments reintegrated to one another without shame, derision, or judgment—so that we can once again know and own the truth of who we really are.

Not who the world says we are, or conditions or society or tradition or anything, just the *yes* of Love for ourselves.

May we start by offering freedom to ourselves and then move into offering freedom to others in relational connection.

By scarcity's standards, it is impossible to ever be enough.

This seed of discontentment serves as the greatest asset of capitalism in inducing a panic-filled, anxiety-ridden society trapped in the hustle while constantly perpetuating lies we believe:

1. I am never enough.

2. I will never have enough.

The lies we believe and our fears as a society are keeping us in a constant state of torment. We keep doubling down on ways that we are different instead of leading from our common unity (community).

We are afraid of who has more, afraid of who will get in and who will be left out, afraid of our bodies, afraid of other races, afraid to share power, afraid of gender fluidity, afraid to explore our sexuality, afraid to talk about sex without feeling shame, afraid of different religions.

Any expression of living that differs from our own evokes fear and permission to critique those differences as something other than holy or sacred.

Fear of difference demands that we *set the record straight*, pronounce the judgment of *clean* or *unclean,* as if we can see motives of the heart.

Pause.

Close your eyes.

Drop down into that deeper breath.

- How am I obstructing the Way of Love in the life of another through my fears?

- What obstacles to the path of Love am I creating in my own life through ignorance or lack of understanding?

- How am I resisting change by clinging to my fears?

Friendly reminder: I don't know all the things...and neither do you. But that's okay. We're here to love one another with open hands, open hearts. We're here to receive love, to be love, to participate with Love.

And when we are confused about what we know or don't know, we just keep showing up. Clothe ourselves in our own skin, embrace our own warm hearts, and, in the truest form of ourselves that we can gift to the world, we return to who we are called to *be*, and we show up.

Perhaps this is the most generous thing we can offer a world steeped in scarcity and discontent: return to Love and then show up in the world as *be*-ings, not doings.

What God in His mercy has taught the bees
He has not graced the lion or wild ass;
the bee knows how to make a house of liquid sugar.
It is God who opened to him this Way of Knowledge.
What God in His mercy has taught the silkworm
the elephant himself cannot understand or repeat.
—Jalāl al-Dīn Muhammad Rūmī

Sometimes, God, in Holy Three's mercy, opens up a Way of Knowledge just for you.

And the lesson the Holy Three has for you is just for you.

Where some go awry is taking a lesson meant specifically for them and offering it to the general populace as an interpretation and way of life for all to live by.

Deconstruct the web built by a thousand other voices and interpretations.

In all of your unique beauty and glory, spin your own tapestry.

In silence, Love speaks.

Open your heart to hear.

All that you touch you change.
All that you change changes you.
The only lasting truth is change.
—Octavia Butler, *Parable of the Sower*[62]

What has changed for you recently?

Whose touch upon your life changed you in ways that are unforgettable?

Did that interaction make you more resistant to change or open to its possibilities?

In what ways do you consciously participate with change?

62. Butler, *Parable of the Sower*.

Tend first to our own suffering.

Our emotions hold wisdom.

What are they trying to teach us?

What is the fear? Where is the breach of trust?

How do we direct our energies most effectively for change?

Howard Thurman taught that the well-being of one is intricately linked to the well-being of the other.

We are all connected.

This connection is not a denial or erasure of the particularities of our personhood, but rather a perichoretic dance of all the energies that make us who we are, inside the flow and life of Love.

Face to face to face, all that is genuine within me is revealed.

Inside that communion, where everything that is opposed to Love's kind is stripped away, where all the voices other than Love's singular *BE* are silenced…there, I uncover what is genuine in me.

There, every false label and unnecessary attachment dies.

There, I am born again,

each day anew, over and over again.

I turn inward, face to face to face.

I join at the table of Love's feast, that I might join my sound in a blended harmony with others who are doing the same.

> *If I hear the sound of the genuine in me, and if you hear the sound of the genuine in you, it is possible for me to go down in me and come up in you. So that when I look at myself through your eyes having made that pilgrimage, I see in me what you see in me and the wall that separates and divides will disappear and we will become one because the sound of the genuine makes the same music.*[63]
> —Howard Thurman

63. Thurman, "The Sound of the Genuine."

WAITING

Wait for the space for your heart to expand.

Wait for the space for your ears to open.

Wait for the moment to lose the "Yea, but…."

Wait for the moment when safety matters,

lives matter,

the moment the witness, word, and integrity

of our hearts

become our transformative practice,

not only our belief.

In the waiting,

be open to the witness of teenage girls,

be a sanctuary for the refugee,

be an open door to dirty field laborers,

without repulsion, suspicion, fear, or mistrust.

Don't rush to believe invented lies

that send people

into the cold with the animals

and creatures of the night.

Be incarnate.

Stand

in solidarity

in mercy

in compassion

in peace and goodwill toward all.

I am constantly challenged in life by one burning question:

Do I trust Love?

Do I trust that Love will lead me, and those I care about, into Love's embrace?

Do I trust the energy of Spirit to participate with Love, even when it seems like I or someone I love is derailing from the path I envisioned?

And what of disappointments? What of the moments and times when people fail me, when institutions I've believed and hoped were safe spaces that represent the Way of Love turn out to not be that?

Broken people, who in their unhealed state project their brokenness onto others, create dysfunctional families and messy institutions—unsafe spaces that lead us far from home.

In the bosom of Love's embrace, I've come to understand that the degree of my healed emotional capacity will always determine the level in which I am present and consciously participating in relationship with others. In the absence of healing, I will choose rightness over relationship and protect my defended self with ferocity every single time.

Love is the foundation for mutuality.

Love is the foundation for safety, wellness, and unconditional acceptance.

Love is the structure in which freedom is governed.

To the extent that I do not trust Love, I will not trust in humanity's ability to live in peace together. To the extent that I do not trust Love, I will not trust that I can find home in the world.

As a Black woman with five decades of living, I've become an expert in reading the comfortability thermometer of white bodies in dominant-culture spaces.

Discomfort is a great deterrent to belonging.

I've learned how to adapt, shrink myself, change my tone of voice and my patterns of speech, diminish myself, or even become invisible to accommodate the discomfort of white bodies.

These are all tricks and tools of the trade to go along to get along. It's a learned coping mechanism, a set of survival skills that aren't taught in school. These lessons are more caught than taught, learned from observing the body language of elders, mothers, and older brothers. They are things you absorb and *just know*, things that are said with the eyes and head nods or things we heard expressed as warnings cloaked in cynicism that's really birthed in fear:

"You smellin' your own piss."

"You thinkin' too highly of yo'self."

"Some places ain't for you."

And yet, this is not the life I want for myself: to diminish myself because of someone else's discomfort with my personhood. I can do it because I have to. But what I most want is to live in a world where the welcome mat for my whole self is laid out. I want to live in a world where space is made for me to exist how I am, as I am, without any threat to my personhood. I want to live in a world where bad gets better, where a renaissance of inclusion and acceptance blossoms. I want to live in a world where fear does not rob us of our freedom to be. I want to live in a world that is safe to call home.

It takes a lot of inner work to get to the place where we can allow ourselves to be the same person no matter the situation or circumstance, to not become a chameleon who changes based on reading the room. I need places to be my whole self: to be seen, to be known, to be valued, to have my voice and self-expression held in concert with others, without any demands of assimilation, conformity, or diminishment.

We all need that. We all need places and people who hold our safety, wellness, and dignity in the highest regard. Even when we are not conscious of its pull, belonging is the thing that drives us.

Can I trust that these people and this place are for me, hold me in kind regard, have the best intentions in mind for me? Where do I belong? Where am I most welcome? Where does bad get better? Where is home?

We are all constantly looking, searching for home.

Home is the place where you are prioritized, where connection with you is prioritized. Home is the place where your heart is handled with tender care. Home is not the place where you are dominated, manipulated, controlled, or required to be anything other than yourself. Home is the place where you are free. Even when your expression of freedom may not be understood, it is still allowed. Space is still made for your choices, your expression—the fullness of your personhood.

How do we begin to come home to one another? How do we participate with Love to create communities of care where everyone is at home in their body and at home in the world?

Establishing home—the lived experience of safety, wellness, and dignity—is an ongoing, infinite process of attentive, intentional care that is lived out day to day as we dance with Love.

Establishing home begins with being honest about what we do not know, waking up to what we are unconscious to, and acknowledging where our perceptions and perspectives have been muddied or distorted.

From a posture of humility, we can see what we need to unlearn and where our actions have been harmful and our words have erected barriers to establishing a welcoming home for ourselves and other bodies.

Establishing home begins with inner work: healing our wounded inner child who fights with such ferocity to protect and defend herself, the one whose natural inclination is to choose right over relationship, to guard her heart with anger and rage, to choose retribution as a form of protection. How do I come home to her? How do we come home to ourselves?

For me, it all begins and ends with Love. Love is the Source, the Ground of All Being. Love is the deep source of wisdom within, the fount of our life energy. To find my way home to myself, I have to find my way home to Love. To establish home in the world, I must first establish home in myself.

How do I become a welcoming, inclusive person? How do I move to a posture of unconditional acceptance instead of judgment?

The capacity to become who we long to be already exists within each of us. We are, after all, created in the image of Love.

We all bear the *imago Dei* in our personhood; *per sonar*, the holy innocence or Thurman's *sound of the genuine* sounds through each of us. Even when we're doing stupid sh*t and participating with destruction, creating chaos instead of safety, the *imago Dei* does not change. The truth of who we are does not leave us. Michelangelo once said his job was to carve away the excess stone that hid the finished work. What stonelike edifice blocks us from seeing ourselves clearly?

Much of who we are, the truth of our being, lives whole and intact, unmasked, beneath the layers of our defended selves—the excess we protect.

With lots of patience, the practice of stillness creates room for unearthing the truth of our being. There in the quiet, we learn to trust—Love, ourselves, and, finally, others.

Trusting Love changes how we see and what we are willing to allow. Trusting Love is the path that leads to establishing home.

People hurt you. I get that.

They do dumb sh*t. I get that too.

They live their life incongruent with the words they say.

I see that.

They blame-shift. I see that too.

But can I encourage you?

Don't live *your* life in reaction to *their* character defects.

There is so much wonder and beauty, treasure and depth

beneath that tough exterior you try to display.

I see you steeling your heart against the pain.

I see your fear spilling over into sabotage.

Just know, you can hold on to the certainty of pain,

the fear of *what if*

or

you can choose to let go and risk being vulnerable and trusting.

It's okay to soften your edges.

And one other thing:

It's not necessary to put folk on blast all over social media.

You be for something rather than against it.

You find the message of love that is teeming with life and live it.

The greatest act of freedom is you being fully you as you allow your heart to be wholly governed by Love.

Hey, heart…

Is this costing me my power?

Is this costing me my psyche?

Is this costing me my soul?

Do I feel confused on some deep level?

Am I physically drained to the point where I feel like I'm losing life?

Am I compromising the integrity of who I am?

To whom have I yielded my permission? What do I need to reclaim?

Hey, heart…what do you want me to know about me?

Relationships that remain at the surface level never develop the depth of love necessary for trust to form.

Where there is no depth or relational capital to keep me invested, conflict causes disconnection and withdrawal.

If I don't know that you love me or have my best interests at heart, it's difficult for me to trust you.

Trust is rooted in love, in the belief that you care, and in focused attention and affection.

Hostility and prejudice are often fueled through scarcity mindsets and the idea of self-protection these propagate.

Let's start with rebuilding trust. Let's try our hand at doing life together. Let's have coffee, share a meal, or go for a walk so I can hear your heart, and you can hear mine.

Act with integrity and intent in ways that say: "I'm here. I can't make you trust me. I can't make you feel safe with me, and I'm not going to perform for your trust, but I'm going to be intentional about learning what I don't know, unlearning things that may have caused harm, whether intentional or not, and showing up beside you as I do my own work."

As our hearts are changed, our behavior will reflect that transformation, and we will mirror lovingkindness to one another.

Love is being safe enough to communicate what you need and how you feel while allowing the other party to respond to your needs in the way they choose, not the way you expect or demand.

AND...

Sometimes, you are so swallowed by overwhelm that you can't begin to articulate what you need or what you feel.

I get it. I am the world's worst at advocating for myself, specifically when it comes to needing others to adjust to accommodate my hearing impairment. I often feel embarrassed or belittled when people laugh because I've asked them to repeat what they said or I misunderstand what they've said, and these embarrassing social miscues cause me to withdraw into isolation.

This leads me to people who battle depression. I wonder how difficult it is to self-advocate for something that's so hard to put into words.

You cannot know how painful it is to long to hear the birds chirp or converse in the car with your kids and not be able to do so.

For the hearing community, these things are taken for granted every single day.

Mirroring the pain of my own needs, I'm reflecting and thinking about how much I take for granted in my sanity.

How difficult is it for us to understand because we have not stood under the weight of mental illness? What aspect of your life might be a window, a mirror, a place where you could relate to the ills of another?

May we hold one another with great care and compassion.

Allow compassion and sense of self to coexist.

I can care for another person's problems without losing myself in my concern for the other

and

I can maintain a sense of my boundaried self without having to cut myself off from another or disregard their pain.

Love is not divided.

Love is whole.

The pain of rejection, abandonment, or even being misunderstood is that you feel insignificant, unworthy of being chosen, unworthy of the time and commitment it takes to pursue knowing, to pursue truth.

The outworking of said pain can manifest as a deep ache that takes years and years to heal.

Honestly, I'm not sure we ever fully heal from it.

But I do believe, with Spirit's help, we can change the energy enough to recognize when we're being swallowed within the swirl of that pain.

Love is like a lifeline, a tether.

It is always pulling us toward wholeness.

In the throes of a trigger, touch your heart center and say:

I am worthy.

I am significant.

I am worth being chosen.

And even when no one else will,

I will side with Love and participate in my wholeness.

I choose me.

If my self today could offer any piece of advice to the wounded, the broken, and the hurting, it would be: Don't be afraid of your pain.

Don't force it away.

Don't rush it away.

Journey with Spirit inside of your pain. Allow Spirit to bring Truth and healing.

We've been so programmed to cast out darkness that we forget evening and morning make one whole day.

Love is just as present at night as in the day.

Life doesn't have to be polarized into all or nothing.

I've learned that if I rush my pain or dark emotions away too quickly, I miss the opportunity to learn.

May healing love bring wholeness.

Never fear.

Pain will not consume you.

KENOSIS

We are all fed by something that has emptied itself, Beloved.

Why resist?

Surrender.

I'm not asking you to change, Beloved.

I'm asking you to surrender.

Surrender initiates alchemy.

I am faithful and true to the Dance.

Will you participate with me in the process?

Surrender.

Our injured egos often remain attached to the outcome of our stories and the perception and opinions of others.

When people and situations fail us, we feel disrupted, violated, put upon.

That attachment or entanglement seeks to right itself by wielding control until our ego returns to a place of comfort. That's all justice is, really: right alignment.

Healing requires a reckoning, acknowledgment…and, to some degree, or maybe even to a large degree, a letting go.

Detachment releases the authority of external things and dead weight that does not serve our well-being.[64]

---

64. Adapted and expanded from Caroline Myss, *Entering the Castle: Finding the Inner Path to God and Your Soul's Purpose* (New York: Free Press, 2007), 92.

According to Brené Brown, an SFD (shitty first draft) is the story you tell yourself before you rumble through it enough to get to the edit.

Ernest Hemingway said, "The first draft of anything is shit."

In stillness, pause and ask your heart, "In what way has fear changed me? What's the echo of fear resonating in my heart chamber at this very moment?"

If you can handle the answer without beating yourself up, you'll see it for what it is: a shitty first draft.

Grace and truth are realized in Love. Just follow it through.

Don't stop at the SFD. And stop bringing out the lash to punish yourself every time you have an SFD.

We all do it, but the alchemy happens when we acknowledge those voices, the emotions, and the pain, and wrestle through the story they are attempting to weave.

Feel all that intensity and then pause, listen to Love's voice, receive Love's truth, and say *yes* to it.

Give your heart room to take it all in.

Learn how to tango through the web of the SFD into the resonance of Love that breeds confidence for your heart. There's the resting place. Sometimes getting to rest takes a little bit of hard work.

That's the joy of both/and. No dualism or extremes there.

And remember, be kind and patient with yourself in this space. As Jen Hatmaker once said on her podcast *For the Love*,[65] we don't need to hustle through our story.

---

65. jenhatmaker.com/podcast.

The work of dismantling domination begins with the recognition of value.

Acknowledging value leads to acceptance and inclusion.

Acceptance leads to freedom.

If I do not recognize my own value, I'll constantly

compare, compete,

count and measure,

size up the other,

attempt to edge out any perceived competitor

without acknowledging our interconnectedness

or the ways we each have been gifted with uniqueness of person-hood to serve and benefit the whole.

What is your offering?

How does love pour through you?

Do you recognize the value of Love in another?

Can you allow for freedom of expression in all its variations and differences?

To the degree that we don't know we're loved, we cannot trust.

The wisdom teacher Jesus modeled trust for us when he said, *"Father, into your hands I commit my spirit."*[66]

Who do you trust enough to surrender your *chi*, your energetic life source, to?

Whose love is so unwavering, steadfast, and resolute that you can fully surrender without fear of harm or being wronged?

All breaches of trust are cracks in the foundation of love.

---

66. Luke 23:46 (NIV).

Sometimes, we'd rather choose messy than alone,

and sometimes we're so numb to our own habits

we can't see a way apart from them.

We resign ourselves to bad because we've never experienced better.

Child of Divine Love, you weren't meant to be a doormat.

Child of Divine Love, you weren't meant for a life of constant pain, betrayal, and harm.

Remember who you are, Child of Love. Remember who you are.

Have you ever read *Cane* by Jean Toomer or *The Invisible Man* by Ralph Ellison?

Have you ever perpetrated a fraud in life, presented an illusion of yourself to the public eye?

Winning on Facebook, Twitter/X, and Instagram while killing yourself softly on the inside might be such fraud.

Have you ever just outright lied and created another persona to fit in while longing for someone to know the real you?

Not you? Never.

Stop for a moment. Lose the stones.

In some form or another, we all have given in to deception and partnered with a lie.

There was grace for you. Give grace to others.

Arrogance comes from ego—facades and false images presented to the world as my best self—and has its roots in pride, "I know best."

Confidence is born of love.

In Love, I live, move, and exist. Love is the origin of my self-worth.

As I agree with what Love believes about me, I walk toward the truth of my being:

I am valuable.

I am significant.

Rooted and grounded in Love, I know what I can do and what I can't do, what I will do and what I won't do.

Others may not always agree with my actions or decisions, and that's okay.

I am not responsible for the judgments or opinions of others.

I cannot control what someone else thinks or how they will respond.

I choose to look for what Love is doing and follow.

Because I am safe with Love, I allow myself to be guided,

even when others don't understand,

even when I don't understand.

Even if the journey propels me into luminous darkness, I trust Love.

There is freedom in Love.

Love has taught me
   to live free
   to let my *yes* be *yes* and my *no* be *no*.[67]
When I need to explain my actions to another
   often
   it is because my ego is seeking their approval or
   affirmation,
When I need to justify my actions,
   often
   it is because my ego,
   knowingly or unknowingly,
   is afraid of the judgment and/or censorship of
   another.
Whatever decision you make for you,
   inside of your relationship with Wisdom,
   be free enough to own it.
You owe no one anything,
   above living loved.

---

67. See Matthew 5:37.

When agreement is the goal of communication instead of understanding, we will automatically close our heart and our ears to any viewpoint that we disagree with.

As we work on maintaining a high view of humanity, not shutting down and tuning people out, we can stay engaged and listen as a way to honor others and allow the beauty of their authentic expression to rise to the surface.

In a world where many are mad, angry, and volatile, we need strong truth with kindness and empathy.

May we be the kind of people who can say, "I don't necessarily agree with you, but I want to hear your perspective."

Be the kind of person who is moved with compassion.

Be the kind of person who shows up and loves those others don't or won't love.

Be the kind of person who stands in their truth without ostracizing anyone else for theirs.

We are all on a journey home to Love.

Home for me is not a physical landmark or geographical place I return to.

Home for me is wherever Doug is, the place where love overflows.

Home is being present with any one or all of our kids, or any random combination of the four.

I Home is being with one or all of my *sangha*, the women with whom I spend hours on end, talking freely about every imaginable thing under the sun. The place that's free from censure or restriction.

Home is one-on-one conversation with a dearly loved one,

an exchange of meaning on social media,

an excursion with a friend and her daughter.

Home for me is rooted in people:

People who give themselves freely to me and allow me to be free with them—chest bared, fully alive, safe to be my truest, rawest, craziest, deepest, most conflicted self.

Relationships break people open all the time.

People are both beautiful and hella messy, myself included. Love never coerces nor forces.

Unconditional acceptance is the freedom to love without bias, judgment, fear, control, or the need to change or manipulate.

And so I pray: "I have not responded in the light of love. Fear and frustration won today. As I pause to consider Love, make yourself known to me. How do I love the people who are in my life right now, even the ones who may not understand me or agree with my actions?"

While it is important to realize all the mitigating factors that go into the choices and decisions we make, getting to choose is a sacred act.

Agency is no longer living someone else's ideas about how we *should* exist and take up space in the world.

Agency is determining what most aligns with the core values of our authentic self and choosing for ourselves what is best for us.

For me, part of reclaiming choice as a sacred act is choosing how I respond when the little girl inside is triggered. Better still, I'm learning that I have the agency to depersonalize my reaction to the actions of others because the reality is oftentimes people aren't doing something *to* us; they're just doing it.

The freedom I value so much for myself is only as beautiful as the freedom I choose to extend to another.

Even when I disagree with someone's choices, I still believe in letting grown folx be grown and giving them the freedom to make their own choices. Consequences are masterful at teaching any life lessons that need to be taught when we don't rush in to save, fix, or rescue.

Despite having a high value for freedom of choice, I don't manage myself well when people try to *make* me. My amygdala registers all attempts at control as a sign to fight or flee. Sometimes I have both defensive responses at the same time, which then actualizes in knee-jerk texting, FaceTime spewing, or cutting myself off from the world and stomping to my bedroom, wine bottle in hand, like a petulant child trapped in an adult's body.

Then there are moments when, instead of drowning my frustration about things beyond my control, I leave the wine bottle on the nightstand and opt for crying. I allow rage to course through my body, giving myself the freedom to curl against Doug's pillow.

What a win: feeling my feelings instead of numbing them.

Life happenings are an invitation for me to consider love, to decide for myself what I can do and what I will do, to take a step back from the melee and decide how I want to show up in authentic fidelity to myself when the *shoulds* happening around me do not align with my core values.

This is my journey. I will not always be known or understood by others, and that is okay. I have to live in my skin, and I can't do that in an authentic manner if I betray myself.

The act of punishing is easy and mindless. Addressing harm by harming removes the need to think critically and consciously about repair and accountability.

For the wounded inner child (and the grumbling adult) who very much wanted a mothering love free of harm;

for the child who wanted a love that saw, that held, that embraced;

for the child who needed to be nurtured and comforted and never was, may you come home to Love, home to yourself.

May you learn new ways so that patterns aren't repeated.

May forgiveness be a requiem for your pain, and Love's embrace a solace for all harm.

You may never have gushy stories to tell or fond memories to hold, but you can heal.

You can thrive. You can flourish.

You can create a life of love that is sacred and whole.

It will require you to show up for yourself in yourself, to expose the hidden for healing.

But it is worth it—*SO* worth it.

Hang in there, wounded inner child. These moments are to heal, not to shame; they are for your freedom.

May all that weighs you down be released, and in the fullness of Love, may your heart be set free.

Like the birds in the sky and the eagles flying high, may you fly free.

After reading *Eve*[68] by Paul Young, I find myself trying to put into words a reality Love has impressed upon my heart. If there is no absence of light or shifting of shadow, and Love and I are face to face, I see no void at all. The only way I see a shadow is if I, in my own choosing, turn my back on the light that is being emitted. The only way I sense the absence of light is if something blocks that light.

As I pondered the thought, I realized this revelation is as true about my relationships with people as it is about my relationship with Love. When people wrong me, wound me, frustrate me, or irritate me—or insert any emotion of negation—I turn away in my heart. And in the turning, I'm no longer seeing that person through the

68. William Paul Young, *Eve* (New York: Howard Books, 2015).

light of the strength and beauty of our relationship *or* through the light of Divine Love and what the Holy Three believes to be true about that person or the Divine.

It is there, in that place of turning away, that the accuser of people comes alongside with whispers and vain imaginings to cause doubt, mistrust, and disconnection to grow in our hearts toward the other person, or toward Love. And as we continue to turn our faces away from the light of Love, lies are strengthened and empowered by our agreement and judgment toward the other person.

However, when we choose to remain face to face, despite discomfort, our eyes remain clear, and our whole body is filled with light. In that place, we can see the truth of brokenness—ours and theirs—without expectation or demand of repayment for something they have no capacity to give. We do not have to be in denial about the brokenness and character defects of a person, but Love invites us to see as Love sees, to draw strength from the grace and vulnerability. I've heard it said that we are dung-covered diamonds. Without denying the dung exists, Love invites us to see beyond it to the diamond that lies beneath.

I understand why God has no illusions. There are no shadows to create them.

When I become the judge of another and declare evil in action and intention, I turn my heart and face away from that person and partner with accusation.

By believing my own lies, I unleash and empower a violent, lying terror that walks alongside me as a constant companion, providing colored lenses, walls, accusations, judgments, and fists full of stones. Its power is so great, I forget the good of another's heart. And in exchange for the security provided by its blanket of anger, I lose the power of love.

May there be no place in our hearts for accusation and division.

We, as a society, stay believing the lie that we can control others. And it's telling in our demands, expectations, and noisy opinions of how others *should* respond, what they should have done to *make* someone else behave—as if we could ever *make* someone do something. On a good day, we're all doing one hell of a job just to control our own personhood and direct the vision of our own lives in this dance with Love.

Be careful of the assumptions we make and the blanks we fill in when we don't know all the pieces and parts or have the full benefit of being in the room. It's a story we tell ourselves that is fixated in what we believe should or shouldn't have happened.

When we're not aware of the drama being played out in the quiet of our own heads, we unconsciously give ourselves to its inner turmoil, which spills over into our reality, often playing out in relational tension as blame, shame, manipulation, fear, and control.

No one has the full history of another person's inner turmoil and why or how they react to their silent drama raging within. This is why radical empathy and compassion are more necessary than judgment.

There, by the grace of God, go I.[69]

---

69. See 1 Corinthians 15:10.

People hide their sh*t because we, as a society, don't handle the public exposure of people's messy parts well. Too often, we use our words, opinions, and judgments to join the accuser in shame, blame, guilt, and *should haves*.

Trust that while drag queens, pop icons, celebrities, and others in the media whose lives we comment on may never read our cruel words, our friends, our family, and the people in our sphere of influence will.

Shame causes people to hide.

Think about it. How hard did you kick against the goad? Will your people want to expose the worst of themselves to you? From your actions, will they trust that you are a person who can handle them with care, or will they expect to be roasted, filleted, and laid bare?

Social media has us fooled about our roles in life. Bearing witness to suffering, ills, and tragedies does not mean we have been called to be judge, jury, and executioner.

We are invited into the Way of Love to be active participants in life's mysteries. This invitation requires discernment—wisdom tempered with mercy, compassion, and kindness.

Love beckons us to participate as healers, as Good Samaritans who allow themselves to be inconvenienced. Who will take the weary, the wounded, and the injured to the inn for respite and pay of their own funds while they recover?[70]

Friends, don't grow weary in doing good.[71]

---

70. See Luke 10:29–37.
71. cf. Galatians 6:9.

The one thing I ask—of my kids, myself, and anyone else I've ever had the humbling experience of leading or pastoring—is to give me the grace and permission to evolve and change.

Some things I believed with such great fervor ten, fifteen, even twenty or thirty years ago, I no longer hold as true, or I no longer hold onto them as tightly as I once did.

For the times I parented or pastored with an iron hand from a place that has since shifted, I've had to ask forgiveness.

The biggest sin of my life has been the sin of certainty coupled with the pride of "I know best."

The greatest gifts Love handed me were: the grace to live deeply in mystery; the freedom to say, "You know what? I don't know"; and the ability to be completely at home and at rest in not knowing and not needing to know.

After the dust settled, I realized more than anything that I wanted to be a person who loved people more than I loved my credo. Kudos to anyone who can admit they kinda, sorta, maybe didn't have it all right. I know I definitely didn't.

And that brings me to you, dear reader.

At some point in someone's life—your teacher, your parent, your pastor, etc.—they had some thoughts, wrestled some things out, figured some things to be true.

And this is not to discount what was true to them or for them where they were at that moment in their life—when their lived experience, coupled with the wisdom and wrestling of the lived experience of their mentors, helped them form the thoughts they arrived at.

Those ideologies, beliefs, fears, hopes, etc. were then passed down to you as wisdom or truth, idioms and expressions. You did not have the benefit of knowing how they arrived at that piece of advice. It became, for you, the law, the bedrock of your belief system, and how you've formed every thought, every decision, and fashioned your way forward.

But there comes a time when you have to recognize that for what it is—the ways you've been taught—and then trust yourself to measure your life your way.

Does that mean we cut off all the wisdom, beliefs, and truths that have been shared with us? Absolutely not.

It means we honor that information, that formation, while realizing there may have been some cracks in the foundation.

Free yourself to forge your own way.

Allow yourself room to evolve.

Change. Question.

In doing so, some wisdom will stick, some wisdom will morph, and some will fall away altogether.

You can include and still transcend.

You can be the owner and creator of your own life without completely abandoning or cutting off what you've been handed.

Freedom is being able to define yourself for yourself while owning every part of what makes you fully alive and fully human.

Authentic power is holding your own tools, your own keys, and participating within Divine Love to craft the narrative of your own life, not one that's been handed down to you from someone else's past relationships, experiences, and/or religious interpretations.

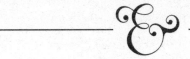

People can't validate you when they haven't done the work to validate themselves.
—Dr. Nicole Lepera

W hen we realize that most of the parenting we received was just our parents mimicking the parenting they received (good and bad), we can let that be what it is and figure out how to:

+ Relate to ourselves differently

+ Relate to our own children differently

+ Separate what we believe from what our parents believe

+ Figure out our own values for our own unique lived experience.

This is not rebelling against tradition. This is honoring *what is* while still evolving.

Receive those things that mirror Love and invite you into wholeness, then release the rest without personalizing or internalizing it.

Every human wants to be seen, heard, and given the opportunity to fully express themselves.

Most adult humans, expressing their brokenness and stunted behavior, have an inner wounded child that was not given an opportunity to be.

Pause.

Remember what you needed, what you perhaps didn't get…or maybe you did.

The next time you are graced with the honor of being in the presence of a small sacred being, offer them the gift of being seen and heard, and allow them to fully express themselves.

Our world will be better for the gifting.

Motherhood. You spend the first part of it not really knowing what you're doing...or perhaps that was just me as a young adult mom.

And because you're still in the first half of life yourself, all your parenting is geared toward trying to *make* your kids behave according to the moral code you've been handed.

But really, underneath that aspirational behavior modification is your own wrestling with the opinions of others. "What will people think of me if my kids are unruly?"

And so, you're stressed AF most of their toddler, preschool, and early adolescent years, living for the clock to stroke the magic hour of whatever time you've deemed is right for bedtime, according to all the childrearing books and opinions of grandmommas, aunties, and church mothers.

And it feels like never-ending years of butt wiping, nose wiping, and teaching them how to pee in the pot without getting so much of it on the floor.

But time has a way of moving life along. And somehow, you move from the stressed-out early years to carpooling and chaperoning extracurricular activities—dance, sports, debate, forensics, you name it, there is something for your child to do. And so you're eating dinner at 9 p.m. or, God forbid, 10, just to eat dinner as a family.

But oh, the laughter and the stories. And you wouldn't trade it for the world, except...

Teenage years bring a different kind of stress and, dammit, enough time hasn't passed, enough healing hasn't happened, and so you're still caught up in the machine called the *opinions of others*, and so you yell and scream and punish and take away privileges because "What will people think?" and "Oh my God, they might die or get killed or, God forbid, get arrested!"

And then, somehow, without killing them or dying yourself of a stress-induced heart attack, they graduate high school and leave home, so it's quiet. Super quiet.

And you're a lot less stressed, but still stressed because college is hella expensive and parenting young adults away from home brings a different kind of *I can't control them* stress, so it's still stressful, but not like the stress-of-the-past-eighteen-years stressful.

But quiet, yeah. And different.

Because eighteen years of your life has been butt wiping and laughter, nose wiping and laughter, screaming and yelling, but definitely laughter, hours upon hours in the car and sitting on hard-ass bleachers, but laughter and cheering and so much laughter.

And all of who you are has only been a mother, and you know no other part of yourself outside of this identity, which is its own existential crisis. So you'll either dig your heels in and continue to try to mother like you did for the past eighteen years, or you'll shed the skin, retire the title, and learn a new rhythm of life. And you can say *yes* to that, or fight against it with mad resistance, which only leads to major depression. Don't ask me how I know.

And so, you surrender—what you thought mothering was, how you mothered, your identity as mother.

But...it's quiet. And you have to learn a new way of being.

Then they come back to visit. And all that you've shed finds its way back, and you're cooking again, and laughing again, and doing all the mothering things.

But now they're adults, old enough to share a beer, and it's no longer stressful because you no longer give a damn about other people's opinions, and you no longer are convinced that behavior modification worked anyway, except to create the illusion of perfection, and so you're just here, being present, enjoying the humans your once-small children have morphed into. Enjoying the laughter and smiling inside at how the thing that brings you the greatest pleasure is watching each of these beautiful creatures come into their own as their authentic, unique selves, despite all the ways you tried to squash them and mold them and make them fit into the tidy package Christianity said was good and righteous.

Now you know.

Now you know that they are sacred and holy and worthy because *they are*, not because of you or your eff-ups or any single thing you think you did.

It is because they came into this realm full of beauty, truth, and goodness, and somehow, in spite of you, not because of you, they too have learned to move beyond the praises and approval of another person's opinion and have learned to start living to the beat of Love that resounds in their own hearts.

And this…this is when you breathe deep and soak in the majesty of being a mother.

If you were a parent who raised your kids saying, "I'm not your friend. I'm not your friend," don't expect to enjoy a friendship with them later in life.

Friendships are about knowing and deepening a shared space built on trust and mutual affection.

Rather than focus on what you're *not* with your children, teach them how to navigate boundaries inside of relationships.

This lesson will transcend the parent/child dynamic and go with them as they evolve and grow.

If you never model friendship with boundaries, mutual affection, the reciprocity of giving and receiving, and being heard and listening, how do they learn soft skills for adulthood?

We can still be friends and have boundaries for respect, for conversation, for how much is shared, when things are shared, and how they are shared.

I had the potential in life to be anything I wanted to be. I chose to be *Mom*. Now that my kids are grown, I have the potential to remake myself and once again be anything in life I want to be. I choose to be *Friend*. Somehow, I think the win is not in the role; it's in the *Being*.

Be Present.   Be Love.   Be.

Over the years, Love has taught me that just by virtue of being a parent, I'm not owed a relationship with my kids.

Love is not love if it's not freely given.

And all friendship is a gift, even that which an adult child chooses to extend to the parent who raised them.

It took a lot of quiet, a lot of self-reflecting, a lot of owning my sh*t to get to the point where I could detach myself from my kids' existence—their accomplishments, their failures, and their own ideas, ideals, and convictions.

Fueled by the weight of other people's opinions, the need to be right, and the need to be in control, afraid of outcomes that we can no longer manipulate or admit to manipulating, we stay too overly involved in the lives of others beyond what is our place.

And recognizing my own complicity, I've attempted to own my mistakes and my failures, to acknowledge my wrongdoing and the ways in which I've missed the mark.

Parenting adult children and seeing them enter the cocoon that takes them into their next phase of life is gut-wrenching.

The fear of it will drive you to micromanage, helicopter, and use control to attempt to manipulate life to give you the outcome for their lives that feels the safest to you.

But the truth is, as we dismantle the hierarchy of the parent/child domination complex and allow them to take their place beside us in the circle of life, we have to let go.

Be a friend. Be an ear. Listen. Love.

Offer help when it's desired, but, even more importantly, learn to receive from them as equals. Surrendering to their adulthood allows for mutuality and exchange.

My head knows this. Still, my heart echoes these words:

Watching your children go through the hells of life offers a small glimpse into what the heart of Divine Love must feel like when people suffer.

It's so easy to make our child's pain about us—our failures, our ineptitude, or what we could've, would've, should've done.

But Divine Love never does that. The Holy Three climbs inside our tragedies with an all-consuming love, offering hands, eyes, heart, and commingling tears as Love weeps with us, sits with us in our pain, loves us, and ultimately guides us from the place of pain and suffering into a place of healing and peace.

In an effort to rescue and protect, we often want our kids to skip the step of feeling their pain, forgetting that beauty comes after the ashes and joy after the mourning.

There is no resurrection without death.

Let healing have its perfect work and don't rush the process.

Sometimes the only way to joy, according to Jesus, is to endure the cross.[72]

Too often, as parents, we try to continue parenting adult children with the same sense of hierarchy and dominance of power that we lord over our small children while rearing them, and the model doesn't work.

Dominance breeds disconnection, distance, and secrets.

With everything in me, I try to grant my *kids* the freedom to be their same selves with me as they are in any other setting.

I don't want them to learn two-faced hypocrisy at my expense.

But I also understand that permission relinquishes my right to demand relationship.

When the hierarchy is abolished, the relationship shifts to one where each participant is 100 percent responsible for their part of maintaining connection.

They get to choose.

---

72. See Hebrews 12:2.

Familial obligation is off the table when Love leads because love always recognizes the gift of choice and honors another's freedom to choose.

I do not force myself upon my kids. I'm not a mom who does all the things or does them well. But I have tried to dismantle the parent/child hierarchy and make myself available for friendship.

I seek to offer the gift of listening, being, holding space, and making memories, laughter, and celebration.

At the end of the day, I want friendship because another person wants friendship with me, not because they feel like they have to, by rule of some antiquated sense of familial obligation.

I'm an all-in kind of friend, and I can love to the point of consumption.

But isn't that true of the fire of Love? Fire warms. Fire burns. How we participate and receive from that fire often determines the difference. Too much, and something that was once soothing and comforting becomes a roaring inferno, burning everything in its wake.

My heart is not to consume that which came from me, extends out from me.

It is to be the fire that warms when the air is chilled, to be the coals that roast the marshmallows just so, creating memories birthed of anticipation and delight. It's to be the heat that warms stiffened and frostbitten fingers.

How does the fire of Love radiate from you?

Are you aware of the ways in which your fire can erupt and become wild and uncontainable?

How do those you love receive your love? What does it feel like for another to stand within the warmth of your love?

Sitting at the gas pump at Sam's Club, I watch the angry momma, the sullen child. I hear their angry words rise unbidden through the air. My insides twist. I remember being the child...and then, painfully, I remember being the momma. And I write:

For all the days I fussed at my kids,

I'm sorry.

For all the times I didn't remove the scowl from my brow

when I looked at you,

I'm sorry.

For every time I embarrassed you in front of your friends,

I'm sorry.

Sometimes the pain leaks,

and we don't know what to do with it,

aren't equipped to hide it

or heal it.

All we know to do is transmit it,

unaware of the damage it causes,

the distance it creates.

We perpetuate disconnection,

participating with disillusionment.

For the ways I failed to heal you,

I'm sorry.

For the ways my anger and violence created your brokenness,

I'm sorry.

"If only" doesn't change the past,

but I pray acknowledgment of my wrong

will be the release you need

to heal,

to be.

For every Momma in pain,

your kids see your eyes,

they hear your scold.

It feels like hate.

It makes them question their existence.

It sends them running to alternative forms of affirmation and approval.

It's the seedbed of doubt.

Heal, Mommas.

Love, Mommas.

Be honest about your pain, your past, and your wrongs, Mommas.

And most of all, Mommas, let's ask forgiveness for the ways in which we've been complicit in fracturing our young.

And then return.

Return to Love.

Return with Love.

Return with an olive branch.

Return armed with forgiveness.

No more harsh words,

hard brows,

back slaps and "Do that's."

Return with Love

and offer the gift of your whole, healed self.

Conditions and transactions are neat, controllable.

The guidelines and expectations are clearly measured and defined, providing a sense of comfort and safety.

The ego, given the opportunity to flex and perform, thrives well amongst conditions and transactions.

We have learned to live conditionally or transactionally, which eliminates the need to live relationally.

Relationships are never neat. They are as messy and varied as the people who bring their whole multidimensional selves to exchange and participate in life with one another.

But people are worth it.

You are worth it.

One of the greatest lies we've ever bought into as a society is that our ultimate end is to be happy and win at all costs.

It has stunted our ability to sit with and be with. It has buried the sacred act of lament.

We numb hard times with whatever form of escapism suits our whim or fancy. Rushing through painful moments, we aspire to *just move on* and *get over it* without honoring what life is gifting or teaching us.

If we resist our hard, painful moments of suffering or despair, we condition our hearts to believe life is to be conquered, not lived.

From the beginning of time, we've seen humanity's natural inclination to fix, to resolve.

We rescue, we save, we swoop in like heroes and, in so doing, we rob people of Love's invitation to journey with Presence through life.

Relationships are hella messy.

There is no getting around the highs and lows of living, and the only way we journey is through.

The question is, do we numb ourselves to the pain and the mundane, only coming alive for the adrenaline rush of life's thrills and roller-coaster highs, or do we stay awake for the whole of it?

There will always be a little child inside of us longing to be loved, longing to be invited and included.

For the most part, wounded people do not have the capacity to love our inner child the way we desire to be loved.

This is where forgiveness and Divine Love become crucial for healing and moving toward wholeness. The wonder of Love is that its healing power creates enough spaciousness within to allow our hearts the room they need to free ourselves from attachments, grudges, and expectations.

The moment I chose to stop hoping someone would love me in ways they were completely unable to and said yes to joining where Love was working, I witnessed the knotted threads on the underbelly of relational tapestries unravel in the Divine's hands.

I'm a witness that broken things can be made whole.

I want to hand my family freedom:

You will be afraid, and you will experience joy.

This is the beauty of your humanity—that through

every emotion, through the highs and lows of every

experience, you do not have to fragment, separate,

or cut yourself off because Love is always present.

Love has no opposite, not even fear. Love is whole.

If I can gift my family line the freedom to live whole, to live loved, whether afraid or joyful, we will be able to embrace our humanity without illusions of perfection as the ultimate be-all and end-all of our existence.

No feeling requires fixing.

With Love as our anchor, we can be alive and present to what we feel—even fear, even joy.

Don't ever become so enlightened that you lose sight of people.

One of the things that remains attractive about the wisdom teacher Jesus is the way he included.

You can't teach me anything if it's not rooted in Love—

+ Not nationalism
+ Not certainty
+ Not theological interpretation
+ Not German philosophy
+ Not spiral dynamics
+ Not even critical race theory

How are you living Christ? How is Infinite Reality, the Ground of All Being, expressing itself through you? How are you participating with Love?

You can be as smart as Einstein, as holy as the pope, as woke as Angela Davis...but if it does not bear the mark of Love, it's all dung.

Love is the structure in which freedom is governed.

Like riverbanks,

I may splash my freedom against the shores,

but my dance with Love keeps me conscious of the spilling

so I can manage myself well.

When I love you,

my freedom is harnessed for our mutual benefit and flourishing,

not for selfish purposes.

So much of life isn't going to turn out how we thought it would be.

How do we cope when the imagined pictures of our expectations do not match the lived reality of our daily existence?

Do we withdraw?

Do we become bitter?

Do we try to wrangle life into conforming with our demands, as if it ever would?

Do we say *yes* and surrender to what is?

How do we evolve and adapt to life when things don't go as planned?

Blessed are the flexible, for they will not be bent out of shape.

When discomfort arises, when faced with choices and opportunities, I often touch my heart and remind myself that this too is an invitation.

But here's the thing about an invitation: We get to choose how we respond.

Just because we're invited, doesn't mean we always say yes.

It means we get to choose.

And our choice is a powerful, sacred act.

Even still, when Love invites our participation,

there is always beauty for ashes[73] in the Divine exchange.

---

73. See Isaiah 61:3.

Scarcity breeds desperation,

causing us to invent imaginings.

Fear of not having enough leads to

hoarding,

distancing,

other-ing,

and all kinds of narratives to justify our selfishness

And validate our decision to choose self-protection over generosity.

Difference is not an obstacle...at least, it doesn't have to be. Difference is an invitation into knowing.

Deep breath.

Touch your heart and say:

I am experiencing discomfort, but I will resist the desire to flee from this moment.

Love is with me.

I can be afraid *and* curious at the same time.

I do not have to allow my fright to invoke flight.

I will stay present—to my own discomfort, to the moment, and to what or who is different.

May we marvel at the beauty of our differences and not be afraid.

What happens when we finally get what we want?

Sometimes, we can live in such a defensive posture that we forget what forward movement feels like.

Unlock your knees.   Unclench your fists.

Today is today; embrace it with gratitude and a wide-open heart.

Don't miss the beauty of now in your protest of what is not.

It seems all too easy to get sucked into the melee that swirls around bravado and deception.

All the drama, all the fear.

Each side sees things so clearly, yet not clear at all, trapped as we are in our individually constructed realities.

I wonder what happens when more of us move from the middle of madness, distance ourselves enough to bear witness as nonjudgmental, compassionate observers.

What do we do with what we see? How does it inform our lovingkindness?

Does it evoke mercy and generosity, or do we hunker down in our selfishness, convinced that the bootstrap method is the best way to *make it?*

How could unconditional acceptance pave the way for allowing differences to exist and overlay freely without the need for people to see as I see or believe as I believe?

Could such a reality produce symbiosis amongst the masses?

Would that a world existed where all of humanity cared about one another and the issues that affect their lives as deeply as we care about our 401(k)s and investment portfolios.

Would that *"love your neighbor as yourself"*[74] meant more than just the other people in our gated communities and hiding behind ivory towers of privilege.

---

74. Mark 12:31 (NIV).

Would that the trophy of success didn't necessitate the marginalized as losers in order to have a declared winner, that counting and measuring would give way to common union, decency, and dignity.

Emotions unscathed, F-bombs tucked away, I breathe without constriction.

I aspire to believe and hope and feel expectant.

From death, from the bottom, we can rise.

And even when it doesn't feel like any of life makes sense, I trust Love.

What cracks open a seed and causes it to germinate?

Root systems grow in the soil, where it's dark and hidden and there seems to be little air.

Yet a whole lot of life is forming in the dark before the seed ever breaks through the dirt in the form of a sprout.

Life is a little like this as well.

Hearts are cracked open by pain, tragedy, and suffering:

Dying small deaths,

gestating underneath the surface

in the womb of healing,

being born anew.

The sea is calm today.

The water glistens across the expanse.

Boats enter, boats go out,

the blinking lights guiding their safe passage.

The waves crash in a constant song,

the foamy white settling onto the shore,

sunrise hidden behind clouds

and yet the sun rises once more.

Life is like that—calm, glistening.

People go in, people go out,

the light of Love providing safe passage as they journey through this realm of time.

Trouble crashing, landing like foam on the shores of our world.

And yet we are assured that no matter how dark the night,

the sun will rise once more.

Every day I get to choose:

Will I look at the foams of trouble

settling on the shore, fading fast,

or will I look upward, fixing my eyes on the place just between the clouds,

the place where day breaks

and the sun also rises?

A band director takes the stage, calls his pupils to attention, and instructs them all to play middle C.

The note is struck.

Resonance.

Many instruments, one note.

Synchronization: one sound.

He then tells his band to warm up their instruments by playing a chord.

Air expands through the instruments:

many instruments,

various notes,

still one sound.

I admit, as a former band member, I still get a little choked up when bands play chords. There's just nothing like it—

Until…the band begins to play its melodious symphony.

Rich. Striking. Deep in Complexity. Beautiful.

Oh, the diversity of notes, of timing, of instruments, of skill it takes to pull off a symphony.

One note gives us resonance. It centers us, brings us back into alignment.

Many notes give us a symphony. They add value to our expression, our diversity.

We are the instruments through which Love blows.

Like a band director, Love has a high value for diversity.

Love empowers us to explore the world beyond middle C, knowing that the center of our beings holds the truth of who we are.

Love encourages us to explore the cosmos beyond the edges of the chord chart and add our own depth and uniqueness to the score.

Writers often develop ideas about a new story while writing a current one. They may even jot down a few plot ideas and character names. But only when the present story reaches *the end* can an author turn the page and fully embrace the new story.

I think life is a lot like that.

If you've drained the last vestiges of hope from your present story, perhaps it is time to give yourself permission to declare *the end* and turn the page to make space for a new story to emerge.

My Aunt Josephine used to say, "There's only so many ways you can beat a dead horse before you realize the thing is just dead."

But that's the beauty of death…it's always followed by a resurrection. It's why spring follows winter.

Mourn the end, if you need to, then embrace the new.

Don't be blinded by what you know to be true
because of what you want to be true.
Listen to your own inner knowing.

Acceptance is not the same as being *okay* with something.

Just because I have accepted something…

(It is as it is. It is what it is. I release my need to fix. I release

my need for this to be different. I release my desire to control

or wrest this situation into fitting my desired outcome.)

…does not mean I'm okay with it.

I can very much disagree and be at odds

with a decision and still accept it.

This is the beauty of contemplation.

It builds within us a spaciousness to hold both/and.

But thinking someone is *okay*

because they've accepted something

dismisses us from fully considering that person's feelings

and opinions about their experience or the situation.

The caterpillar does not fight its way into the chrysalis's cocoon;

it yields to the process.

There in the womb of luminous darkness,

swaddled in grave clothes,

what was fades away.

Present to Death, present to the intimate immediacy that is

beyond all illusions, imaginations, or expectations

it does not think of what is to come.

It burrows itself in Rest.

There is only what is.

Wholly immersed in death's shroud,

accepting it fully,

then...

and only then

emerges what is to come:

Flitting beautifully, majestically into new life.

AWE

Awe –

the color of the sky over the sea at dawn or dusk;

the shape and place of a tree;

the sound of hummingbirds or tires slapping

against the pavement in the rain.

Awe –

the wrinkles of a newborn, fresh from the womb:

smooth feet, wizened eyes.

Awe –

a coyote in a neighborhood or a roadrunner

running back and forth across the street.

Awe –

the New Mexico Sandias, snowcapped or bare.

What catches your breath, causes you to pause and take notice?

What enraptures you, enveloping you into its existence—even for a small moment?

What picturesque scene or moment in time invites you to forget about yourself, the places you have to be, the things on your to-do list?

Awe is all around, deep-hidden springs of beauty laid bare when we are present to the moment, present to one another.

How do we reclaim it, make time for it?

In our hurried, fast-paced world, where too many of us live trapped in destination disease, it's easy to miss the invitation of awe.

Paul Young once said that every person is a burning bush, and when we encounter another, we should treat them with awe and wonder, for every human being is holy ground.

The beauty and radiance of Love shines clearly in nature. And yet, sometimes it feels much harder to see it shining as clearly in ourselves or in another.

Why is that? Why is it so easy to see wonder in nature but not in humanity?

Perhaps it's because we see nature as an object under our dominion—something for us to control and manipulate, something we can use, consume, and toss aside.

Perhaps it's because we're more prone to see people as competition—the measuring stick by which we compare and rank our worthiness.

Comparison keeps us from seeing beauty.

What if, instead of comparing and measuring ourselves, we used those moments to look for beauty, to search for the wonder in another?

The proverbial measuring stick of *enough* robs the moment of its awe—good enough, fast enough, smart enough, talented enough, enough money, enough connection…

Am I enough? How does my enough compare to your enough? How can I get my enough higher up on the totem pole?

Counting and measuring—and all the gesticulating and posturing that come with their demands—rob us of the capacity to be awestruck by one another.

Our capacity to wonder, to be awed by life, is only as big as our ability to be present in the present moment and present to one another.

If my attention is in multiple places at once, how do I really see beyond a glimpse? To what am I giving myself when I am not fully present in the present moment and present to others?

Even the very act of living, moving, and having our *be*-ing, which Rob Bell calls *the I AMness* of the human experience, holds awe and wonder.

Life is pure, sacred, holy.

The whole of you living fully in your body is pure, sacred, holy.

Acknowledging this is the beginning of awe and wonder.

I am pure. I am sacred. I am holy. I am wonderfully made.

Can you be awestruck with yourself? Not in an arrogant, conceited way, but in an *I am the "very good" of creation, made in the image of Love*[75] way. "My body is good. My heart is good. My mind is good. I get to be alive today, to be a part of the universe. I get to give myself in love and care for the betterment of the cosmos."

How can we be awestruck by anything around us if we are not awestruck by the miracle of our own existence? We are all mirrors and invitations. The good that you see in me is a mirror to the good that is in you. And where you cannot see your own beauty, truth, and goodness, my being is an invitation for you to sit with Love and allow those parts of yourself to be unveiled.

While some say we are dung-covered diamonds, I like to say we are all art projects being restored. That first look may not evoke a sense of awe and wonder, but what will the long, loving gaze reveal?

All of creation is the face of Love expressed throughout the world around us, including you. You are beauty incarnate. Do we look upon one another and see that beauty, or have our eyes become dim to the reverence of our being?

---

75. See Genesis 1:31; 1:26.

The Scripture that comes to mind, not for its contextual accuracy, but for its lyrical poetic gleaning, is Genesis 28:16:

Then Jacob awoke from his sleep and said, "Surely the LORD is in this place, and I did not know it."

What have we missed because we've been asleep, or looking at our phones or screens?

I think one of the gifts of the COVID-19 pandemic, racial uprising, and political unrest has been more of us awaking from sleep.

We are seeing with our eyes, noticing one another, and pausing to see, to speak, to hold the door open—expressions of intentional kindness.

We are realizing that life is not promised. We are stopping to smell the roses, take the hike, go kayaking, and find wonder in the midst of hell

Our skin sheds cells and regenerates. We breathe without thinking about it. The sun rises. The sun sets. There is wonder in every day.

Awe creates within us a sort of spaciousness for vulnerability, a place to hold the unguarded moments of bared souls so we can receive the gift of another's unveiling without trampling or soiling their reveal. We don't run from their wonder.

"You are safe with me," creation—our first Bible—teaches us.

Nature lives its life out loud on full display, not in spite of us or for us, but with us. It doesn't care who sees it. It's unapologetic and inviting. It's provoking and hallowed.

Through a brilliant sunset behind a mountain range, or dawn turning to day as the sun rises above the roar of waves crashing along the shoreline, geese in flight, snow-covered meadows, toadstools in Utah, or acres and acres of forests, nature teaches us about the pregnant pause, the expected transition between labor and delivery, where life is birthed—messy, naked, and unashamed.

Flowers are unafraid to die when their season has come to an end.

Trees share their branches as homes for others, modeling cooperative living.

These moments of awe and wonder are not just there for sentimentality's sake.

They are gifts. Pregnant with lessons, they are our teachers.

"I want you to see me in all my glory," nature seems to say.

With such sheer intensity, the mutual knowing makes us want to kneel and kiss the ground. Burning bright to catch our attention, awe of the sacred within another beckons us to turn aside.

Easy to spot in nature, how do we miss that same overwhelming, breathtaking beauty in one another? When has the face of a friend moved you to tears with the wonder of their beauty?

Awaking from our sleep state, awestruck by their beauty, we wonder, *"Surely the* Lord *is in this place, and I did not know it."*[76]

Wonder keeps our heart open to love. It's the place where our defenses are lowered.

If someone were to ask me, "How do you find God?" I'd suggest a walk among the redwoods, a trip to the Grand Canyon, a blanket on the beach at sunrise, a hike through the Costa Rican rainforest until you reach the waterfall, witnessing a mother giving birth, or sitting with a wise old grandmother and listening to her stories.

Do anything that opens your chest, expands your heart, fills your lungs with air on a deep inhale, and brings your walls completely down. This openness—this is the place of union, the thin veil where we know we are one with all things.

This place is as different for you as you are different from me. And that's the beauty of it.

Wonder creates space to know that we are all being held by Love.

---

76. Genesis 28:16.

May the eyes of our hearts be open to lay hold of and reclaim that which is beautiful in the world and in one another.

May we, like Jacob, awake from our sleep and say, *"Surely the* LORD *is in this place, and I did not know it."*

I was blind to your beauty and wonder, but in this moment... now I see.

Being awestruck is one way we give ourselves to Love. We surrender to the sacred Presence that beckons us to see the holy in one another.

The divine exchange of

a child's laugh

a friend's shared secret

a pup's wet nose

a baby's milk breath

a partner's calloused hands.

May we awake like Jacob:

Truly Love is in this place

and I am awake to its wonder:

a grandmother's embrace

a wizened neighbor's tales of times gon' by

your momma's honeybun cake and collard greens

your auntie's macaroni and cheese

Truly Love is in this place

and I am awake to its wonder:

the sound of the spine cracking on a new book

decanting a full-bodied wine

letting the air hit your long-held pain

Truly Love is in this place

and I am awake to its wonder.

We were made for love,

designed for a life of wonder.

May all that is eternal within us

greet the wonder of this day.

Unveiled or hidden, Love is always there.

In the hell of our deepest despair,

in the high of our greatest joy,

Love is there.

In the absence of correctly phrased theology and the presence of
misinformation,

Love is there.

In strokes of genius and brilliant creativity,

Love is there.

In heartbreak and ecstatic union,

Love is there.

I may say *in* and you say *the*,

distinctions that rankle with the possibility of confusion.

Still…Love is there.

I may bemoan the twists and turns of your journey,

critique the way you're getting it wrong.

Still, Love is there.

Do I trust Love with you the way I trust Love with me?

Unveiled or hidden,

do I believe Love faithful enough

to bring into alignment all that is misconstrued?

Do I trust Love to make whole

that which is broken,

or do I remain hellbent on helping it along?

I look at the fish, and I'm overwhelmed by God's creativity. I mean, the Holy Three is genius. So many colors and styles, designs and shapes—such an art form.

And I wonder, why in the world do we constantly try to white-wash humanity?

We make us all the same, homogenize us.

True, we all begin and end in Love.

Love is our genesis. From that beginning rises the beauty of who we are—our colors, our shapes, our sizes, our stripes—the creativity of humanity, of all sentient beings. When we truly see each other through the eyes of Love, it's as beautiful as a coral reef full of abstract fish.

How do we look at the fish and the birds with such awe and reverence and pass by one another with less sacredness?

Oh, Love!

Break open our hearts to see Your creative genius in one another, that we may be overwhelmed with the beauty of what we see.

I, too, am a guilty passerby.

For He Himself is our peace, who made both groups into one and broke down the barrier of the dividing wall, by abolishing in His flesh the enmity, which is the Law of commandments contained in ordinances, so that in Himself He might make the two into one new man, thus establishing peace, and might reconcile them both in one body to God through the cross, by it having put to death the enmity.
—Ephesians 2:14–16

The only side God takes is the side of love.

Love is whole.

Love is sacred.

Perhaps that's why the Beloved did not want Adam and Eve to eat of the Tree of the Knowledge of Good and Evil.

Sides create division.

A metaphorical *line in the sand* is drawn when we take sides.

If I'm on the side of right,

it implies someone else is on the side of wrong.

If I'm on the side of justice,

someone else has to stand on the side of injustice.

If I'm on the side of victim,

someone else stands on the side of perpetrator.

And thus, people are constantly being pitted against one another.

"This is quite sad, isn't it?"

"The end?"

"The way I see it, if something makes you sad when it ends, it must have been pretty wonderful when it was happening. Truth be told, I always felt it a bit lazy to just think of the world as sad, because so much of it is. Everything ends. Everything dies. But if you step back, if you step back and look at the whole picture, if you're brave enough to allow yourself the gift of a really wide perspective, if you do that, you'll see that the end is not sad. It's just the start of the next incredibly beautiful thing."
—Rebecca and William, *This Is Us*[77]

Loss is not always punitive.

Everyone faces loss. It's part of being fully alive and fully human.

Could there be an invitation to something new on the other side of loss?

77. *This is Us*, "The Train," season 6, episode 17. Directed by Ken Olin. Written by Dan Fogelman, Jon Dorsey, and Danielle Bauman. NBC, May 17, 2022.

Can loss lead to life? Is there a thread of Love even in the loss, even when we cannot see our way ahead?

Does Love ever fail?

All things change.

If I lean into change and accept the invitation to something new,

if I open my hands and let go of what I thought should be,

if I open my heart and embrace what stands before me...

what then?

Surrender.

Trust the redeeming power of Love.

Lean in, to the grace of the present moment, the grace for *what is*.

Deep breaths.

It feels like so much loss:

wildfires, tropical storms, politics, police brutality, elections, race deniers, race baiters, the COVID-19 pandemic. Save the Kids. Teach the Kids. Evictions. Joblessness.

So. Much. Loss.

And yet...what now? Surrender.

Look for the thread of Love. Even in loss, grace is ever-present.

Feet to the earth. Deep breaths.

Change welcomes us as we lean in.

In the words of Octavia Butler, "All that you touch, you change. All that you change, changes you."[78]

Even loss, which can feel like its own kind of hell, changes us.

If we remember to look for the thread of Love amid the fiery furnace, we'll see an invitation to something new.

---

78. Butler, *Parable of the Sower*, chapter 1.

Loss is a b*tch.

It grabs you by the gut at the most unassuming time and compresses your insides until sadness tickles the back of your throat.

But I'm learning to feel helpless, not hopeless,

at the same time.

I'm learning to look for Love's abundant goodness

without having any expectation of what that looks like

all at the same time.

Life is happy and sad,

good and full of risks and challenges,

sometimes all at the same time.

Breathe, I tell my soul.

Inhale.

Exhale.

Love has this

...even when I'm experiencing loss.

I don't think small touches are random at all.

In all the winding, unwinding, searching, unraveling, questioning, and restoring of my mired ideas about *faith*, one thing has been and will always remain true: I am one with Love and the One Love sent.

He...She...They...Love...God...Beloved...Trinity...Spirit... Wisdom...Abba...Papa... Mother God...the Holy Three... I'm not trapped in the name; I'm caught up in the knowing.

Love loves me because Love loves me because Love loves me.

Religion may have been ripped from me, leaving an open, festering wound, but no one and no thing can ever upend the anchor that is the experiential love of God.

I've tasted and I've seen, and Love will always be the seal that is set upon my heart.

Have I gone crazy? Perhaps.

But some things will never change, and being enraptured by Divine Love is one of those bedrock truths for sure. (Insert the old gospel song, "I tried him and I know him. Found him to be a friend."[79])

Bottom line: Love is as present in the small things as the big.

Love sees. Love feels. Love hears. Love knows. Love acts.

---

79. The Clark Sisters, "Tried Him and I Know Him," on *Live – One Last Time* (EMI Gospel, 2007).

Just because there is nothing, doesn't mean there is nothing.

Stillness is also guidance.

Love never abandons.

In the quiet, may the eyes of my heart turn toward the sun

and remember

the Light of Life is filled with healing Love.

I am here.

I am loved.

Love's faith in me never wavers.

May I lean into the faith of Love as I am led beside still waters.

There, may my soul be refreshed

for tomorrow is not promised

and today will not come again.

For now, for this day

I choose…

I am loved.

I am here.

A POEM OF AWARENESS

I am alive / I am here / I exist.

I will not shrink myself to fit.

I can take up space without fear of recrimination or backlash.

Love leads me beside still waters.

Love restores my soul.[80]

The light of Love radiates brilliantly from within.

Love's light is a guiding force—my Shepherd, my Anchor.

May I remain consciously aware of Love's invitation to participate in the divine dance.

Love is always at work—in me, in you, in us,

for Love is steadfast, and Love never ceases.

Deep breath, then,

trusting in the perfect work of Love:

Braver. Stronger. Onward. Forward.

May Love lead us and guide us into all Truth.[81]

---

80. See Psalm 23:2–3.
81. See John 16:13.

I want to reclaim my homeland.

To reclaim my homeland is to reclaim the secrets of myself.

And so, I've been thinking a lot about home and about place. I've been thinking about longing and missing and being dis-membered.

I've been thinking about what is well within my soul...and what aches. I've been trying to name what is good and peaceful within me, and why, alongside peace, the world within feels barren, so silent and empty.

I've not yet found the words for any of these things, and so...I've been thinking—thinking about living with mystery, thinking about Love, thinking about difference and complexity, thinking about what is true.

Truth is at home within me, in my being, in my presence. Thus, I have been attempting to turn toward my soul with steadfast care. I'm attempting to expand my awareness, to notice and investigate, to hear the sound of Truth resounding authentically within me—loud or soft, rumbling beneath my breastbone.

I've been attempting to unearth that which lies within—truth, love, me. And sometimes I wonder if therein lies the rub. Could excavation be a work of grace? Is the unearthing not mine to do? How much of transformation do I instigate, forcing change like prodding cattle? And how much is simply the act of being rooted, embedded deeply in the soil of Love, shedding what no longer serves, like autumnal leaves falling from trees?

Like the dross that rises to the fore in a refiner's barrel as metals are purified in fire, is my part only to yield, to surrender to the flames of Love and submit to the burning away of all that resists Love's trans-figuration? How do I participate with Love in this longing for align-ment, longing for reclamation, without wresting full control away from the Beloved?

Oh, Love. Oh, lover, burn away all that hinders.

Oh, Love. Oh, lover, burn within me. Ignite me in Love's flame.

Oh, Love, consume me in passion like the rapturous bliss of lovers, seared by your kiss.

The Beloved runs. Do I give chase, or do I wait till the Beloved draws near?

Like Rumi, in his pursuit of Shams-i-Tabrīzī, I seek to lay hold of all that lights the Beloved on fire. For there, I am convinced, within the flames of the Beloved, are the secrets to my reclamation and the answers to my longing.

I know the fire will singe me, burn me, consume me. I also know the fire of Love contains the wisdom for my re-membering.

What else is left for me than to be swallowed whole in Love itself? The place that knows the whole of me is living and breathing. The Beloved's love is my homeland. May the Beloved grant me access to the Divine's beautiful face that I might always be tethered there.

Oh, Love; oh, lover. Beyond Love's sacred name, there are no words for this yearning. Of no place and every place, Love finds me there. In my longing and restlessness, in my desire and discontent, the Beloved bids me come.

Through the night watch, I seek my Beloved. In the luminous darkness, we commune. Mended, pieced together once more by the Beloved's kiss, my faith in self, in life, and in humanity is renewed.

As the sun rises and the new day dawns, life emerges once again: the first day of a new life: new beginnings, new opportunities. Satiated by my Beloved's tender embrace, I am not as lost or lonely. I feel alive—aware, awake.

Every day begins anew: Every new day is the first day of a new life, with new opportunities to do anything.

But sometimes I wake in despair, memories of Love's flame receding to the recesses of my mind, and I return listlessly to my routine: the missing, the longing, the ache.

I do the same things over again—unseeing, unthinking, unfeeling, numb. Thus I cling, trying to remain ablaze, senses sparking, coated with the dew of the Beloved's Love.

As the dew fades from the grass's blade, memory of my love encounter gives way to life's happenings.

Love is not meant to be held tightly.

Love and I meld so deeply into one another, we become. We are integrated, a part of. Love is not found outside myself.

Thus, there is nothing to hold onto and everything to receive.

That is the reclamation of my homeland, the secret of myself:

The Beloved and the lover are one.

Contemplation is awakening to the contemplative dimension of life. Every development in contemplation reveals more and more of the mystery of silence and the importance of receptivity over effort, especially in prayer. Contemplative potential is an innate gift to everyone...It is the capacity to gradually unfold into intimacy with God. God is a relationship: a relationship that has no end and unlimited possibilities. Only by entering into union with God can we learn who or what the self is. God is trying to awaken and free us from unconscious negative motivations.[82]
—Father Thomas Keating

May Love permeate even the deepest parts of who we are and awaken and free us from all unhealthy and unconscious motivations.

May every illusion fall away in the light of Truth.

May the desire to hustle and strive for the sake of image, appearance, competition, and comparison bow its knee to the reality of Love's validation.

For the silence itself reveals that nothing outside of Love will ever fully satisfy.

82. Thomas Keating, *From the Mind to the Heart* (Temple Rock Company/Peter C. Jones, 2017).

A PRAYER OF CREATIVITY

Holy Three, you are the Master Artist.

With strokes of love, you painted the world and all therein.

Everything came into being through Christ, and apart from Love, *"nothing came into being that has come into being."*[83]

Together, the Trinity danced upon the deep and created the world

May we look upon ourselves with kindness and respect for your creative genius.

May we look upon humanity with awe and reverence as we admire your artistry.

May we endeavor to pick up our paintbrushes and join you on the canvas of life to paint:

harmony where there is tension,

unity where there is discord,

peace where there is turmoil,

love where there is fear.

May each stroke connect our hearts to you and to one another.

Amen.

---

83. John 1:3.

Love aims its fury at all that is opposed to Love's kind intention toward us.

Exposure is an opportunity for healing and alignment.

In the fire, dross rises to the surface to be sifted, removed. What remains is pure gold, as is each of us.

Imago Dei.

The heat is on, and the pressure is high.

"In this world you will have trouble,"[84] says the wisdom teacher Jesus. The question is: Will we endure the discomfort long enough?

Only Love knows the *kairos* moment to sift the wheat from the tares, to skim the dross.

"Take heart," Jesus reminds us. *"I have overcome the world."*[85] Domination and conquering are not our work.

Our work is to love, to surrender, to trust, to be.

Our work is the work of participation.

---

84. John 16:33 (NIV).
85. Ibid.

There is no formula to life and freedom.

Love invites us to dance.

Love is the ultimate transformative power.

Wholeness happens inside of Love, not apart from it.

Walking out the process of wholeness takes

time,

trust,

surrender,

consent,

willing participation,

trial and error,

and gut-busting honesty.

Love leads to a thriving life, transformation of our hearts, and flourishing. Love is the source of healing.

Wholeness happens inside the knowing and the receiving of Love.

How that happens varies from person to person because each person is unique.

To dance with Love—our guide, our healer, our partner, our teacher—is the ultimate invitation of life.

This is eternal life, that we might know Love and the One sent to incarnate Love.[86]

---

86. See John 17:3.

Immanuel: Love-with-us enrobed in flesh.

Where the spiritual, ethereal, and otherworldly is embodied and made manifest in the physical realm,

Christ has come again.

May we accept with peace and goodwill Love's invitation to dance.

We must proclaim the truth that all life is one and that we are all of us tied together. Therefore it is mandatory that we work for a society in which the least person can find refuge and refreshment...You must lay your lives on the altar of social change so that wherever you are, there the Kingdom of God is at hand![87]

A PRAYER OF SURRENDER

Dearest Love,

Thy kingdom come.

My kingdom go.

Spirit, teach me to lay aside every falsehood that keeps me from walking in Truth and to release every agenda that contradicts Your kingdom of love, including nationalism and selfishness.

---

87. Howard Thurman, "Religion in a Time of Crisis," Garrett Biblical Institute Commencement Address, June 7, 1943.

I surrender my idea of life for Your life, that it might flow freely out of me to the world around me.

May we remember the *least of these*, not in a system of hierarchy or counting and measuring, nor with pity, but for their full humanity.

May we learn to be in awe of the person before us, the one beside us—in the way we vote, in the way we make room, in the way we live and move and have our being.

Where Love leads, may we follow.

Amen.

Dearest God,

When the truth of who you are is fully revealed, may we know that you are not a gaslighting God. You are not a tyrant. You are not a bully. You are not deceived or given to illusions.

More than gaining understanding of what you're not, may we know who you are and what you're for.

And may the fire that reveals, that lights the way, burn away everything that stands in the Way of Love's greatest reveal:

LOVE.

And may we mirror all that we see when we truly behold you as you are. May the truth of our being match the Way of Love.

May we

    wonder a world

    where peace reigns and love wins.

May we

    be carriers of hope

    to participate with Love

    in bringing such things to the world around us.

May we

    look at the state of our nation

    and see more wonder and hope

    than grimness and despair.

In the face of our own truth,

    may our compassion toward one another

    be rekindled.

May it be so.

There is in every person an inward sea, and in that sea there is an island and on that island there is an altar and standing guard before that altar is the "angel with the flaming sword." Nothing can get by that angel to be placed upon that altar unless it has the mark of your inner authority. Nothing passes "the angel with the flaming sword" to be placed upon your altar unless it be a part of "the fluid area of your consent." This is your crucial link with the Eternal.[88]

Be kind, dear world.

To yourself and to others, be kind.

While we push and prod and force our way into power and prestige, our hearts are crying for the tender, compassionate touch of the feminine.

When the scales shift too far into a patriarchal land, the use of excessive violence explodes.

Let the feminine grace within remind you to be soft when life says muscle up and be hard.

Return to the center, dear one.

Be centered, beloved.

It's not one or the other; it's both/and.

---

88. Howard Thurman, "The Inward Sea," *Meditations of the Heart* (Boston: Beacon, 1999), 15.

And—the unforced rhythms of grace.

And—the bridge to our re-turn.

And—the thread of Love that binds us to one another and to the world.

And...

Peace be with you. Ashé.

ACKNOWLEDGMENTS

No man is an island, and neither is the process of bringing a book to fruition. While many of the words in this book sprung forth from stillness and solitude, the finished product is a labor of love that could only happen with the help of several doulas, midwives, and labor coaches: Katie Christian, foreword writer extraordinaire, thank you for the gift of your words and your willingness to ensure that readers who might not know me personally see more than an *angry Black woman* wielding a pen. Shirin McArthur (www.shirinmcarthur.com), my brilliant editor for this project, thank you for making my words shine and the opportunity to learn and grow as I bore witness to your talent and skill. Jonathon Stalls (www.intrinsicpaths.com), creator of the stunning, contemplative ink drawings that accompany my body of work, thank you for saying *yes* to someone you didn't know and for pulling me into your creativity. To be seen and to be known through your images is an amazing and humbling feat. To my early endorsers, thank you for taking time out of your busy schedules to read the book and offer your support. To the team at Whitaker House, Christine

Whitaker, Amy Bartlett, and Peg Fallon, thank you for taking a chance on me. Thank you for your belief in this book and for championing and stewarding the message within with kindness and grace. I am grateful the Divine brought us together on this journey.

To you, dear reader, for the gift of your time, your financial investment and belief in me, my heart offers a deep bow of gratitude for your willingness to sit with these words. Thank you.

To Doug, you are my air. To Brittany, Tre', Chaya, and Jeremiah, you are my everything.

AFTERWORD

AND[89]

And teaches us to say yes

And allows us to be *both*-and

And keeps us from *either*-or

And teaches us to be patient and long suffering

And is willing to *wait* for insight and integration

And keeps us from dualistic thinking

And does not divide the field of the moment

And helps us to live in the always imperfect now

And keeps us inclusive and compassionate toward
everything

And demands that our contemplation become action

And insists that our action is also contemplative

And heals our racism, our sexism, heterosexism, and our
classism

And keeps us from the false choice of liberal *or* conservative

And allows us to critique both sides of things

And allows us to enjoy both sides of things

And is far beyond any one political party

And helps us face and accept our own dark side

And allows us to ask for forgiveness and to apologize

And is the mystery of paradox in all things

And is the way of mercy

And makes daily, practical love possible

And does not trust love if it is not also justice

And does not trust justice if it is not also love

And is far beyond my religion versus your religion

And allows us to be both distinct and yet united

And is the very Mystery of Trinity

—Fr. Richard Rohr, OFM

89. "And" was first published in *Radical Grace*, April–June 2008, vol. 21, no. 2. © Center for Action and Contemplation. All rights reserved. Used with permission.

ABOUT THE AUTHOR

Felicia Murrell is a certified master life coach and former ordained pastor with over twenty years of church leadership experience. She has spent several years serving churches and training others in various inner healing modalities with an emphasis on helping people become unencumbered to the cares and burdens of life that keep them from experiencing freedom and connection with the Divine.

Felicia also serves the publishing industry as a freelance copy editor and proofreader. The author of *Truth Encounters*, she resides in Woodbury, Minnesota, with her husband, Doug. Together, they have four adult children.